IMPLEMENTING
PROBLEM
BASED
LEARNING
IN LEADERSHIP
DEVELOPMENT

EDWIN M. BRIDGES

PHILIP HALLINGER

ERIC CLEARINGHOUSE ON EDUCATIONAL MANAGEMENT
UNIVERSITY OF OREGON
EUGENE, OREGON
1995

Copyright © 1995 Edwin M. Bridges and Philip Hallinger

Library of Congress Cataloging-in-Publication Data

Bridges, Edwin M.
    Implementing problem-based learning in leadership development /
    by Edwin M. Bridges, Philip Hallinger ; foreword by Joseph Murphy.
       p.   cm.
    Includes bibliographical references.
    ISBN 0-86552-131-X : $14.95
       1. School administrators—Training of—United States. 2. School
    principals—Training of—United States. 3. School management and
    organization—Study and teaching—United States. 4. Problem solving—
    Study and teaching. I. Hallinger, Philip, 1952-   .
    II. ERIC Clearinghouse on Educational Management. III. Title.
    LB1738.5.B75 1995
    370'.7'60973—dc20   95-5124
                                                        CIP

Printed in the United States of America, 1995

Design: LeeAnn August
Type: 10.5/12.5 Palatino
Printer: Cushing-Malloy, Inc., Ann Arbor, Michigan

ERIC Clearinghouse on Educational Management
  University of Oregon
  1787 Agate Street
  Eugene, OR 97403-5207
  Telephone: (503) 346-5043 Fax: (503) 346-2334
ERIC/CEM Accession Number: EA 026 366

This publication was prepared in part with funding from the Office of Educational Research and Improvement, U.S. Department of Education, under contract no. OERI-RR 93002006. The opinions expressed in this report do not necessarily reflect the positions or policies of the Department of Education. No federal funds were used in the printing of this publication.

The University of Oregon is an equal opportunity, affirmative action institution committed to cultural diversity.

MISSION OF ERIC
AND THE CLEARINGHOUSE

The Educational Resources Information Center (ERIC) is a national information system operated by the U.S. Department of Education. ERIC serves the educational community by disseminating research results and other resource information that can be used in developing more effective educational programs.

The ERIC Clearinghouse on Educational Management, one of several such units in the system, was established at the University of Oregon in 1966. The Clearinghouse and its companion units process research reports and journal articles for announcement in ERIC's index and abstract bulletins.

Research reports are announced in *Resources in Education* (*RIE*), available in many libraries and by subscription from the United States Government Printing Office, Washington, D.C. 20402-9371.

Most of the documents listed in *RIE* can be purchased through the ERIC Document Reproduction Service, operated by Cincinnati Bell Information Systems.

Journal articles are announced in *Current Index to Journals in Education. CIJE* is also available in many libraries and can be ordered from Oryx Press, 4041 North Central Avenue at Indian School, Suite 700, Phoenix, Arizona 85012. Semiannual cumulations can be ordered separately.

Besides processing documents and journal articles, the Clearinghouse prepares bibliographies, literature reviews, monographs, and other interpretive research studies on topics in its educational area.

CLEARINGHOUSE
NATIONAL ADVISORY BOARD

Timothy J. Dyer, Executive Director, National Association of Secondary School
    Principals
Patrick Forsyth, Executive Director, University Council for Educational Admin-
    istration
Paul Houston, Executive Director, American Association of School Administra-
    tors
Joseph Murphy, Vice-President, Division A, American Educational Research
    Association
Joyce G. McCray, Executive Director, Council for American Private Education
Maggie Rogers, Director, Information Center, Northwest Regional Educational
    Laboratory
Samuel Sava, Executive Director, National Association of Elementary School
    Principals
Thomas Shannon, Executive Director, National School Boards Association
Don I. Tharpe, Executive Director, Association of School Business Officials
    International
Brenda Welburn, Executive Director, National Association of State Boards of
    Education

ADMINISTRATIVE STAFF

Philip K. Piele, Professor and Director
Stuart C. Smith, Associate Director for Publications

The Problem-Based Learning Series

Implementing Problem-Based Learning in Leadership Development, by Edwin M. Bridges and Philip Hallinger. 1995.

Problem-Based Learning for Administrators, by Edwin M. Bridges with Philip Hallinger. 1994.

PBL Project—Time Management: Work of the Principal, by Edwin M. Bridges. Instructor and Student Editions. 1994.

PBL Project—Write Right!, by Edwin M. Bridges. Instructor and Student Editions. 1994.

PBL Project—Leadership and School Culture, by Philip Hallinger and Barbara C. Habschmidt. Instructor and Student Editions. 1994.

For more details and ordering information, please see pages 193-94.

Dedication

To Brother Blue aka Hugh Morgan Hill, who taught us that "Seeing and hearing are believing, but eating is knowing."

About the Authors

Edwin M. Bridges is Professor of Education and Director of the Prospective Principals' Program at Stanford University. Prior to joining the faculty, Bridges held academic appointments at the University of California, Santa Barbara; the University of Chicago; and Washington University, St. Louis. He is a former Vice-President of the American Educational Research Association. His current interests are teacher evaluation and problem-based learning.

Philip Hallinger is Associate Professor of Educational Leadership at Vanderbilt University and at the Center for Leadership Research and Development at Chiang Mai University. He has published extensively on issues of principal leadership, school improvement, and leadership development. He has served as the director of several leadership development centers and currently directs Vanderbilt University's International Institute for Principals. His current interests focus on international issues in school improvement and the cultural foundations of leadership as well as problem-based leadership development.

Contents

Foreword

Over the past decade, considerable effort has been devoted to the topic of improving the field of school administration, especially the preparation of educational leaders. Awakened by two influential reform documents—the 1987 National Commission on Excellence in Educational Administration report and the 1989 report from the National Policy Board in Educational Administration—a somewhat complacent profession has begun the arduous task of overhauling its basic infrastructure. The most thoughtful improvement work since that time has drawn its raw material from three sources: analyses of the history of educational administration, critical reviews of status quo, and visions about appropriate foundations for the profession in a postindustrial world.

Improvement ideas have emanated from a variety of quarters and have been promulgated in a myriad of forms. The leading professional groups in the field have been busily engaged in attempting to codify the appropriate knowledge base for a new era of school administration. External agencies like NCATE, the Danforth Foundation, and the Council of Chief State School Officers are struggling to find ways to raise standards across the profession. And throughout the U.S., and in many other nations as well, the faculties associated with preparation programs are at work overhauling the ways they think about school administration and the education of the women and men who will lead tomorrow's schools.

Into this era of ferment and this stream of improvement strategies, Bridges and Hallinger have introduced the notion of Problem-Based

Learning (PBL). Their work is producing, I believe, the most important insights and raw material for the improvement of administrator preparation that we have available for the task at hand.

At first blush, it is easy to characterize this volume—and the other work by Bridges and Hallinger (see especially 1992)—as a new "instructional approach," similar to the development of the case study or the computer simulation. From my perspective, however, this would be unfortunate. While they have certainly and laudably brought a new instructional approach to school administration, they have done something much more profound. At the most fundamental level, with their painstaking longitudinal work on PBL, Bridges and Hallinger have given us a new metaphor for our profession. They are able to grapple with the most deep-seated and intractable problems of school administration in ways that offer real hope of improvement—hope that is lacking in other prominent change strategies afoot throughout the profession.

For nearly half a century now we have allowed our thinking and our action to be shaped by the "bridge" metaphor, the belief that the job of universities is to create knowledge and to construct, or to help others construct, linkages between this knowledge (also known as "research") and the world of practice. A casual examination of the landscape reveals that our efforts to construct these bridges have been largely unsuccessful. A deeper analysis leads me to conclude that these bridges are never likely to be built, and that, even if by some miracle they were, there would not be much traffic on them. The metaphor is wrong. The work it encourages is misdirected.

What Bridges and Hallinger offer us with their PBL work is a new metaphor, which, at the risk of offending them, I would call the "caldron." In PBL, practice and research are thoroughly mixed. While they may enter the caldron as distinct entities, in the cooking—the PBL work—they are blended in processes and products that make recovery of the separate elements impossible. This may be Bridges and Hallinger's most significant contribution. They have redirected our thinking *and* provided a remarkably useful vehicle to actualize this redirected energy. Bridges and Hallinger have found one solution to our most knotty problem—that of the breach between the academic and practice arms of the profession. We would be well advised to mine their work with considerable diligence.

Not only have Bridges and Hallinger forged a caldron where research and practice are blended, but through their PBL model they have also provided a mechanism for the mixing of an array of important learning objectives—many of which are ignored in current preparation programs or, at best, are taught as discrete elements. In accomplishing this feat, they provide us the best strategy available—the most elegant yet parsimonious—for recognizing and honoring the array of beliefs, skills, and understandings needed to be a successful school administrator. I refer here to the very explicit ways the learning objectives are mixed in educational experiences. The PBL activities form the caldron in which, for the first time in my knowledge, nearly all of what we claim is important receives attention. Just as significantly, they are blended in ways that I have been unable to find in alternative instructional models.

What imbues these first two accomplishments with real significance is the way they reorient our thinking about leadership development away from a focus on creating and applying knowledge and toward concern for the development of what Gardner (1993)* defines as *intelligence*: "the ability to solve problems or to fashion products that are valued in one or more cultural or community settings" (p. 7). For some of us in the educational administration reform business, this broader, more powerful focus, while visible for some time, has proved nearly impossible to capture. It is therefore of great significance that Bridges and Hallinger have woven it so centrally into their work on PBL.

The third major contribution of Bridges and Hallinger's work is that it directs attention to, incorporates, and mixes nearly all of the central ingredients of a constructivist-anchored conception of learning and teaching. Again, in a comprehensive and integrated fashion, the authors tackle a set of deep-rooted problems that we have been grumbling about for fifty years, but on which we have made distressfully little progress (for example, passive learning, teacher-led instruction, assessment distally connected to valued activity, a focus on the arts-and-science model of dissertation research, and so forth). In their PBL learning model, Bridges and Hallinger not only overcome many of these weaknesses and create new ways of doing business (for example, student-centered learning, cooperative learning), but, more importantly, they fuse these principles of social-constructivist perspectives on learning into an amalgam that does not lend itself to separation into its more distinct parts. They replace the existing behavioral foundation

---

*Gardner, Howard. *Multiple Intelligences: The Theory in Practice*. New York: Basic Books, 1993.

of learning and teaching with a more powerful infrastructure, and they do so in a comprehensive and meaningful way.

As with all books, there are places where additional information would have been helpful. For example, more discussion on issues such as how one develops the "prerequisite attitudes for problem-based instruction" or how individualized learning can unfold in this cooperative approach would have been appreciated. Two issues, in particular, stand out in this regard. First of all, I believe, more explicit attention might be provided to the educational scaffolding—social-constructivist views of learning—that supports PBL. More specifically, I would have liked to have seen the connections between this model of learning and the implementation of PBL teased out more fully. While I know that these issues are examined in greater depth in the first Bridges and Hallinger (1992) volume,* reenforcement here would have been useful. My concern—based on work on implementation with similarly grounded K 12 reforms—is that it is difficult, at best, to introduce an instructional reform built with constructivist principles into a culture that is defined by another set of principles, especially behavioral ones. I would like Bridges and Hallinger to help their readers—perhaps in their third volume—see this reality more clearly.

Second, more discussion about the lessons that departments of school leadership can learn from switching the basic model of learning would be useful. Throughout this volume, it often appears that the authors are talking to individual faculty members. I often caught myself asking questions about the meaning and implications of PBL for groups of faculty members—for the culture of programs and departments.

These issues are, of course, matters for future work. They detract only on the margins and little at all from the overall value of the book. As I noted at the outset, this is seminal work in pushing and pulling educational administration to its next stage of development. Considerably more than can be related in this short Foreword about the work of Bridges and Hallinger will engage and please the reader. They are painstaking scholars in the best sense of the term. They honor much without glorifying anything. They both think and do. They model

---

* Bridges, Edwin M., with Philip Hallinger. *Problem-Based Learning for Administrators*. Eugene, Oregon: ERIC Clearinghouse on Educational Management, University of Oregon, 1992.

what they value. They think and communicate so clearly that the reader can see and touch the issues at hand. And they push others to extend their work while they continue their own remarkable longitudinal journey.

It is difficult to overstate the value of Bridges and Hallinger's PBL work in helping to reshape our profession. This new volume on the implementation of problem-based learning will be of immense assistance on two levels. Most fundamentally, it provides in a clear and usable fashion the raw material and design sketches necessary to undertake the overhaul of the profession. More concretely, it will allow each of us to begin this much-needed work in our own programs and classes. This is a profound line of work and a wonderful book.

Joseph Murphy
Professor of Educational Leadership
Peabody College
Vanderbilt University

Acknowledgments

We acknowledge the comments of colleagues who were kind enough to read drafts of selected chapters and contribute their ideas toward strengthening the manuscript, including Chuck Achilles, Larry Cuban, Clive Dimmock, Mona Engvig, Ronald Heck, Jan Robertson, Russ Rumberger, Kenneth Hill, and Stuart Smith.

In addition, we note the special contribution made to our understanding of issues in the implementation of problem-based learning by colleagues who have joined this experimental venture, including Patchanee Taraseina, Panomporn Chantarapanya, Umporn Sriboonma, Ruth Greenblatt, Tom Chenoweth, and Bernard Badiali.

We also thank our students at Stanford, Vanderbilt, and Chiang Mai Universities who have showed the utmost patience with us as we have experimented with different forms of problem-based learning in our courses. Special thanks go to doctoral students at Vanderbilt who had the courage to face the risks of being pioneers in their doctoral research on PBL: Barbara Habschmidt, James Jennings, Nedra Wheeler, Eloa Edwards, and Hank Nelson.

Finally, we wish to acknowledge the generous financial and moral support of the Danforth and Walter S. Johnson Foundations. In particular, we have appreciated the constructive suggestions offered through the years by Don Gresso and Peter Wilson.

Introduction

"Problems are learning opportunities in disguise."
Pam Kuhns

Since the publication of our first book on problem-based learning (PBL) three years ago, we have continued to use and refine our understanding of this instructional approach. This second book builds on our experiences in using PBL in a variety of settings and explores in greater depth a range of issues that we touched upon in *Problem-Based Learning for Administrators* (1992).

During the past three years, we have used PBL to teach professors, undergraduates, graduate students, practicing administrators, and those aspiring to be school administrators. Moreover, we have used PBL in a wide array of contexts—week-long institutes, two- and three-day staff development workshops, semester courses that meet on weekends, and quarter-long courses for full-time students. Each of the settings and role groups has presented us with a new set of challenges. By transforming these challenges into learning opportunities, we have increased our understanding of an array of issues inherent in implementing PBL.

Through repeated use of PBL in various contexts and settings, we have sharpened and extended our own thinking about this approach. In chapter 1, we discuss the major components of our most current version of PBL, illustrate how these components operate in the classroom, and contrast PBL with the case method. We also discuss what we have learned about a question that often arises when we work with those who are unfamiliar with this

1

method: How does this instructional strategy impact the content of instruction, the learner, the teacher, and the classroom climate?

As we and others have implemented this approach in the classroom, we appreciate more than ever the importance of the PBL instructional materials and the time involved in developing them. To assist those who desire to experiment with PBL, we discuss in chapter 2 how to reduce the time involved in preparing materials. We also describe and illustrate the template that we have used to develop our own instructional materials, as well as the process that we have generally followed when using this template.

Once instructors have selected or developed their instructional materials, their attention naturally turns to another issue—their role as an instructor. In chapter 3 we examine the role of the instructor by discussing the attitudes, the thinking, and the behavior that characterize successful implementation of PBL. Since evaluation of student performance in a PBL classroom is an especially critical and problematic facet of the instructor's role, we devote all of chapter 4 to this important topic. Our discussion centers on our philosophy of evaluation and the various techniques that we have used to assess student performance.

During the past three years we have begun to explore how PBL can serve to forge meaningful connections among research, theory, and practice in settings other than the classroom. In chapter 5 we discuss and illustrate several options for incorporating problem-based learning into professionally oriented doctoral research projects. The benefits that have accrued to us and our students have exceeded our expectations and have transformed the dissertation into a satisfying and productive experience for students and faculty alike.

As we have moved beyond our own classrooms and tried to introduce PBL to other instructors, we have learned more about the challenges inherent in the change process. We identify these challenges in chapter 6 and the various strategies that we have used for dealing with these challenges.

Throughout this book we have tried to put a face on PBL by conveying salient examples and perspectives in the voices of our students. Therefore, it is fitting that we conclude the book with an essay from one of our students who elegantly discusses "why PBL works."

To those who may be stimulated to experiment with problem-based learning, we wish you the same joy and renewed passion for teaching that we have experienced.

Problem-Based Learning: A Promising Approach to Professional Development

You are the new principal of a middle school where one-third of the 950 students are Latino; 100 of those students are limited in their English proficiency.

Ethnic tensions are mounting; the school is considered "a tinder box." You receive a letter from Mrs. Olsen, president of the "Concerned Parents Group":

> Year after year, these same people continue to expect the United States to support their lack of language acquisition.... Our concern is with the large numbers of such people who bleed all sorts of funding agencies and, generation after generation, never do learn English. The parents never read English books, never watch English television, and never attempt to speak English. Their children are cut from the same cloth; the only place they try to speak English is at school.... Before long these kids from across the border will be classified as "learning disabled" and receive more attention than kids who are serious about their education.... We want you to put these kids in separate classes.

A Latino community leader has a different point of view:

> Latino students don't like coming to school. They feel unwelcome. They sense that the teachers don't understand them and are not making much of an effort to help the students adjust to a foreign environment or succeed in school.... The Anglo students resent the presence of Hispanics and harass, tease, and intimidate them

daily. Overt racial conflict will break out any day if racial relations don't improve.

What do you do?

Messy, real-life problems like these provide the starting point for learning in a radically transformed instructional environment that we refer to as problem-based learning, or PBL. The "students," prospective and current principals, jointly decide how to deal with these problems. In the process of grappling with these real-world challenges, the students acquire the knowledge and skills needed by principals who lead by facilitating collaboration and building consensus rather than by exerting formal authority.

Problem-based learning, though a newcomer to the field of educational administration, has been used for more than a decade to prepare future physicians and other professionals (Boud and Feletti 1991). As one reads about how PBL has been used in these other fields, one discovers that it comes in various forms. This variety stems in part from the differences inherent in the various professional roles for which the students are being prepared.

Accordingly, the version of PBL discussed in this paper reflects the nature of the role that students enact when they complete their professional training in the field of educational administration. This future role, as the reader will discover, influences a host of instructional decisions—decisions about goals, content, instructional process, and evaluation.

In discussing this version of PBL for preparing educational administrators, we elaborate the model, illustrate how it has been used to prepare school leaders, contrast this approach with the case method, and foreshadow what researchers may learn as they study the implementation of this model.

PBL: The Model

Underlying Assumptions

The assumptions underlying traditional preparation in educational administration contrast sharply with those in PBL. Traditional preparatory programs view teaching as transmission of knowledge and learning as acquisition of that knowledge. Program designers for traditional programs make four assumptions about this knowledge: (1) the knowledge is relevant to the students' future professional role; (2) learners will be able to recognize when it is appropriate to use their newly acquired knowledge; (3) application of this knowledge is relatively simple and straightforward; and (4) the context in which knowledge is learned has little or no bearing on subsequent recall or use. Program designers further assume that knowledge is learned most effectively when it is organized around the disciplines (for example, the legal basis for education and educational finance) and taught through lecture and discussion. Finally, those responsible for the professional development of administrators assume that the central purpose of student evaluation is to ascertain whether students recall the knowledge to which they have been exposed.

PBL rests on an entirely different set of assumptions. PBL proponents assume that learning involves both *knowing* and *doing*. Knowledge and the ability to use that knowledge are of equal importance. Program designers also assume that students bring knowledge to each learning experience. Moreover, PBL adherents assume that students are more likely to learn new knowledge when the following conditions are met: (1) their prior knowledge is activated and they are encouraged to incorporate new knowledge into their preexisting knowledge; (2) they are given numerous opportunities to apply it; and (3) they encode the new knowledge in a context that resembles the context in which it subsequently will be used.

PBL teachers further assume that the problems students are likely to encounter in their future professional practice provide a meaningful learning context for acquiring and using new knowledge. These problems supply cues that facilitate future retrieval and use of knowledge acquired during their formal education. Finally, PBL instructors assume that evaluation can play a major role in fostering the ability to apply knowledge if evaluation serves learning (that is, if it is formative) and is based on performance of tasks that correspond to the professional tasks students will face after completing their training.

Major Components

Designing a professional-development program based on PBL requires one to consider five interrelated issues: (1) the realities of the workplace, (2) the goals, (3) the content, (4) the process by which the content is taught and learned, and (5) student evaluation. By attending to these five issues simultaneously, the program designer increases the likelihood that students will be able to transfer their newly acquired knowledge and skills to the work context. Let us examine each of these issues more closely.

Realities of the Workplace

Crafting a program rooted in the principles of PBL involves making a number of assumptions about the realities of the workplace. By way of example, we have adopted several key assumptions in designing Stanford University's Prospective Principals' Program. Local school districts are granting each school more latitude in dealing with the problems and challenges it faces. The principal of the school is expected to collaborate with teachers and parents in solving these problems and in creating an educational environment that effectively and humanely responds to the needs of an increasingly diverse student population. Moreover, the problems and the knowledge base relevant to these needs and problems will continually change.

Goals

In light of the workplace realities that we have assumed, the following professional-development goals for principals seem appropriate:

1. *Familiarize prospective principals with the problems they are likely to face in the future.* Such problems should be those with high impact; that is, they affect a large number of individuals for a relatively long period.

2. *Acquaint students with the knowledge that is relevant to these high-impact problems.* Such knowledge likely comes from a variety of disciplines, rather than from a single one.

3. *Foster skills in applying this knowledge.* Since PBL assumes that knowing and doing are equally important, students should be

provided with opportunities to use their knowledge and to test its utility in dealing with real-life professional problems. In the process of applying the knowledge, students discover gaps in their understanding and in their ability to use the knowledge. This awareness stimulates them to revisit the conceptual material and to solidify their understanding.

4. *Develop problem-solving skills.* Since the character of future problems is somewhat unpredictable, attention must be paid to promoting skills in finding, framing, analyzing, and solving problems. Moreover, future principals need to learn how to distinguish between problems and dilemmas and to acquire strategies for addressing both. While problems generally contain no value conflicts, dilemmas do. Since dilemmas usually arise from competing values, they resist solution and are likely to surface again and again.

5. *Develop skills in implementing solutions.* Consistent with the emphasis on doing as well as on knowing, students should implement their proposed solutions. Simply discussing what one *would* or *should* do to solve a problem is insufficient. Implementation of a solution to a problem often proves more difficult than anticipated; moreover, the solution may bring additional problems. Consequently, principals need to acquire skills in anticipating potential problems, assessing their seriousness, and developing preventive or contingency actions for dealing with potentially serious problems.

6. *Develop leadership skills that facilitate collaboration.* Critical to collaboration are skills in the following: planning and organizing projects, running meetings, achieving consensus, resolving conflict, and listening.

7. *Develop an array of affective capacities.* Unless principals acquire a strong commitment to collaboration and the patience to use this kind of leadership style, they are unlikely to use their skills in working with others. Moreover, when things go awry, principals need to know how to deal constructively with frustration, anger, and disappointment. Above all, they need to acquire confidence in their ability to handle the many facets of this demanding professional role.

8. *Develop self-directed learning skills.* With an exploding knowledge base and ever-changing problems, principals need to acquire

skills in identifying gaps in their own knowledge, in locating relevant resources, and in evaluating the suitability and appropriateness of the resources for the issues confronting them.

Content

Knowledge (content) in a PBL curriculum is organized around high-impact problems of professional practice. PBL adherents follow this maxim: *first the problem, then the content*. Problems are used as the stimulus for learning new content instead of the context for applying previously learned material. One major criterion guides the selection of content. The content should be *functional* in fostering understanding of the problem, possible causes for the problem, constraints that must be taken into account when considering solutions, and/or possible solutions.

Problem-relevant knowledge comes from a variety of sources: the disciplines, the relevant expertise and practical wisdom of practitioners, the policies and practices of the local district, and the students themselves. Although the instructor may suggest pertinent reading material, students exploit an array of sources that may assist them in understanding and dealing with the focal problem—a practice that is consistent with the type of on-the-job learning that PBL seeks to develop.

Instructional Process

In a PBL curriculum, students assume major responsibility for their own learning. The process by which they learn the content mirrors the realities of the workplace and the instructional goals. Accordingly, the process affords students repeated opportunities to practice and refine the skills needed to lead today's schools—skills in promoting collaboration, cooperative problem-solving, and implementation of change.

Unlike traditional educational administration programs, the basic unit of classroom instruction in PBL is a project. Embedded in each project are a high-impact problem, a set of learning objectives, and a collection of reading materials that illuminate different facets of the problem. The problems are usually messy, ill defined, and representative of the problems the students will face as principals.

Students are assigned to project teams that are responsible for framing the problem and deciding how to use the knowledge gleaned from the readings and other resources to deal with it. Each team usually has five to seven members and a fixed period of time—nine to fifteen hours spread over a period of two to three weeks—to complete the project. One of the students is designated as the project team leader; other team members take turns acting as process facilitators and recorders.

Class sessions are treated as meetings of the project team, and the leader in consultation with the facilitator develops a tentative agenda for each meeting. The agenda for each session reflects what the team intends to accomplish and how it plans to proceed. Following each class session, the recorder prepares minutes of the meeting and distributes them to other team members. (See the *Because Wisdom Cannot Be Told* project in Appendix A for an abbreviated description of the leader, facilitator, and recorder roles.)

During each meeting (class session), the instructor acts as "an unobtrusive guide on the side, rather than as a sage on the stage." At times the instructor may raise questions, answer questions, engage the students in reflecting on their process, or provide feedback to students about their use or understanding of the problem-relevant knowledge. If instructors sense that the team is headed in the wrong direction, they do not intervene. Missteps or mistakes represent occasions for learning and often provide valuable insights into the problem, the problem-solving process, the solution, the implementation, the group's functioning, or the students' own sense of self.

Evaluation

Student evaluation, like the goals, content, and instructional process, reflects the realities of the workplace. As part of each PBL project, students are expected to perform tasks and to create products that approximate what they would do while solving the problem on the job. The students' performances during a project, as well as their products, provide the basis for formative evaluation. Accordingly, students receive feedback from peers, the instructor, and practitioners about their performances. When providing feedback to the students, everyone underscores what they have done especially well and raises questions for them to ponder in relation to their performances. Given the nature of the PBL projects, students may receive feedback on their performance relative to any of the eight goals described earlier.

As a way of encouraging students to consolidate what they have learned and to think about transferring their newly acquired knowledge to their future roles, each student prepares a reflective essay at the end of each project. This essay details what they learned and how they intend to use the insights, knowledge, and skills in the future.

PBL: Examples

To illustrate how some of the major components of PBL operate in the classroom, we have chosen two projects, one related to the opening vignette and the other related to teacher selection. The instructional materials for these two PBL projects appear in Bridges with Hallinger (1992, pp. 144-59). A case study detailing what happened during the teacher-selection project also appears in Bridges with Hallinger (1992, pp. 29-57).

Example 1: In English, Please

This PBL project centers on a middle school undergoing transition from a monolingual to a multilingual student population. The vignette at the beginning of this paper highlights several of the numerous subproblems embedded in the problematic situation featured in the project. In addition to the description of this messy, real-world problem, students receive information about the school district, a fact sheet distributed by the school leaders to parents and pupils, and a description of the district's proposed newcomer center for Hispanic students. Students also receive a set of readings that cover such topics as theory and research on bilingual education, translating language-acquisition theory into educational practice, historical accounts of how language minorities have been treated in this country, the legal requirements for limited-English-proficient students, and the needs of recent immigrants.

Members of the project team are responsible for developing a packet of materials to be circulated to the school's Bilingual Advisory Committee prior to its first meeting. The team is expected to include the following materials in this packet:

1. a statement that describes the committee's charge

2. a tentative plan for how the committee should proceed to accomplish its charge

3. an agenda for the meeting that clarifies what the content and the process will be for the meeting

4. a two-page statement that attempts to provide committee members with pertinent background information about bilingual education

At the end of this fifteen-hour project, the team presents its packet of materials to a group of bilingual program coordinators and principals of linguistically diverse schools. This group of practitioners reads the same problem and background material that the team did, reviews the materials prepared by the project team, and meets with team members to raise questions and to provide feedback on the contents of their packet. Team members also have an opportunity to ask questions about issues that arose during the project.

Example 2: Teacher Selection

In this PBL project, students serve on a teacher-selection committee. The committee has been appointed to fill a vacancy for a fourth-grade teaching position. Committee members are furnished with information about the school, the teaching position, and the district, including the teacher-evaluation system. Besides this background information, committee members receive reading materials on a range of related topics—recruitment, theory and research on employee selection, legal aspects of selection, treatment of new teachers, and misassignment.

Committee members design and implement a selection process for choosing the fourth-grade teacher. Since the district requires its teacher-selection committees to interview and to observe demonstration lessons before making a recommendation, the committee must incorporate these two procedures into its selection process. During the last phase of the project, the committee interviews three "finalists" for the position and observes each of them teaching a group of twenty pupils. These students closely resemble those who will be in the teacher's fourth-grade class.

Following the interviews and the demonstration lessons, the committee meets to evaluate each candidate against the criteria it established. When the committee completes its deliberations, it prepares a report to the personnel director that contains the following: (1) the recommendation of the committee, (2) an overview of its selection process, (3) a justification for its recommendation, and (4) a description of the steps to be taken to ensure that the candidate succeeds once hired.

At the conclusion of the project, committee members receive feedback from two sources: the three candidates and the faculty. Unbeknownst to the committee, a faculty member has interviewed each of the three applicants immediately following the selection activity. The interview probes questions like these: If you were offered this position, would you accept it? Why? What did the committee do that you especially liked? How might the selection committee improve its process? The faculty member later shares the answers to these questions with the members of the selection committee. During this feedback session, committee members learn whether their preferred candidate will accept the job offer. This information stimulates the committee to reflect on its process and how it might be improved in the future.

PBL and the Case Method

In our discussions with professors who are unfamiliar with PBL, we are often asked how it differs from the case method. Providing a definitive answer to this important question is difficult because there are several different versions of both methods. Given the variety that exists, we have attempted to clarify the similarities and differences between these two instructional approaches by developing a matrix that highlights the features of our version of PBL and one of the most common versions of the case method. This "Defining Features Matrix" (table 1) can be used to analyze one's own classroom instruction, as well as other variations of PBL and the case method.

These two methods have several features in common. Both use reality-based, problem-centered materials. In PBL these are described as *problems* while in the case method they are referred to as

TABLE 1

Defining Features Matrix:
PBL and Case Method

	PBL	Case Method
Problem-centered	x	x
Student-led teams	x	
Emphasis on analysis	x	x
Class time scheduled by students	x	
Basic unit of instruction: project	x	
Emphasis on implementation and experiencing consequences	x	
Teacher-led discussion		x
Problem a starting point for learning new content	x	
Basic unit of instruction: case		x
Instructor unobtrusive guide on the side	x	
Formative evaluation based on realistic job-related performances	x	
Emphasis on life-long learning skills	x	
Emphasis on problem-solving skills	x	x
Emphasis on meeting-management skills	x	
Emphasis on project-management skills	x	
Concern for emotional aspects of leadership and getting results through others	x	

cases. The PBL problems may be presented in various ways—written cases, vignettes with limited information (additional information supplied in response to students' requests for specific data), filmed episodes, and real-time problematic situations. As with the case method, PBL places considerable emphasis on developing analytical, problem-framing, and problem-solving skills.

There are numerous differences between the two methods, however, particularly in relation to goals, content, process, and student evaluation. In addition to emphasizing analytical and problem-solving skills, PBL emphasizes such goals as the following: life-long learning skills, meeting-management skills, project-management skills, and problem-relevant knowledge.

The approaches to content in PBL and the case method also differ. In PBL, the problem determines the content (relevant theory and knowledge); as we stated earlier, the guiding rule is "first the problem, then the content." If content is introduced in the case method, the theory or conceptual material is presented first. Students are expected to apply these concepts to a case that has been chosen because it lends itself to analysis using the conceptual material introduced earlier.

Perhaps the most dramatic difference between PBL and the case method is the process of instruction. In the case method, the basic unit of instruction is the case. The instructor typically leads the class in a discussion of the case and asks probing questions students are expected to answer. In PBL, the basic unit of instruction is the project. One of the students serves as project leader; the team sets its own agenda for each class session and schedules how the time will be used. The instructor serves as a resource and remains unobtrusive during most of the class session. Students, not the instructor, direct the discussion.

Another important difference between the two methods is the nature of student evaluation. In PBL, as we have noted, the evaluation serves learning and centers on performances like the ones students will encounter in their future professional roles. Students in a PBL classroom do more than analyze and say what they intend to do to solve the problem. They actually implement their solution in a realistic, though usually contrived, situation and experience the consequences associated with their preferred course of action. Throughout the process, they receive feedback from their peers and practitioners, as well as the instructor. Under the case method, students typically prepare a written analysis and statement of how they would deal with the situation. They ordinarily do not put their solution into effect and experience the consequences associated with implementing it. The instructor evaluates the student's analysis and solution.

PBL: Foreshadowed Outcomes

Since PBL represents a radical departure from the traditional way in which school administrators have been prepared, one question often arises: How does this innovative instructional strategy impact the content of instruction, the learner, the teacher, and the classroom climate? To provide a partial answer to this important question, we draw primarily, though not exclusively, on our own experiences with this approach. Thus far, most of the research on PBL has been conducted in the field of medical education, not educational administration. The most comprehensive review of research on using PBL to train future physicians appears in Albanese and Mitchell (1993).

Classroom Environment

Our rendering of PBL creates a more intense learning environment than in traditional educational administration programs. This intensity stems in large part from the project nature of the PBL curriculum. Project teams work without the active facilitation of an instructor; the facilitator, as we mentioned earlier, is one of the team members. Moreover, teams must reach consensus on how to deal with the problem and are required to implement their problem in a context similar to the one they will encounter later as administrators. Although the context is contrived, the vast majority of participants do not experience it as such. Rather, the context has the "feel" of the real thing and that "feel" produces a rather high level of performance anxiety.

Learner

Despite the more intense and stressful PBL classroom environment, participants report high levels of satisfaction. They also view their leadership preparation as much more realistic, practical, and meaningful than their counterparts in traditional programs. However, when asked, "Would you like the portion of the curriculum that is taught using PBL to increase, decrease, or remain the same?", students consistently answer, "Remain the same." According to them, PBL is too intense to be increased and too valuable to be decreased. (PBL occupies roughy 40 percent of the curriculum at Stanford.)*

In a PBL environment, students often learn more than formal knowledge, the kind of knowledge emphasized in traditional leadership preparatory programs. Some adopt or adapt new perspectives on leadership. For example, following a project, one student wrote:

> At the beginning of the project I had little confidence in participative leadership. I doubted that a group could efficiently produce a product in a timely manner using consensus. . . . I gained a new perspective on the role of the leader. Midway through the project I realized I was feeling very stressed about the project. I felt I must determine the "right" answer and then sell it to the group. Reflecting on this, I concluded that wasn't my responsibility as the leader. Problem-solving was the group's responsibility. . . . I can improve (as a leader) by continuing the participative style I tried in this experience—an agenda open to revision by the group, decision-making through a mixture of consensus and majority-rule, equal participation of group members, meeting closure with a review of accomplishments, and followup actions. (Bridges with Hallinger 1992, p. 70)

Still other students learn how to deal with disappointment and the importance of balancing the demands in one's life. By way of illustration, one project leader wrote:

> As to pressure and priorities, I give too much authority to external authorities—bosses, assignments, and so forth—and so lose sight of people priorities outside of the job. To be specific, during this experience I sacrificed my family relationships at a crucial time (for them). This was irresponsible. . . . I have to learn how to put the job in better perspective with the rest of my life and with the world context. Furthermore, by making the assignment and my

---

*See Bridges with Hallinger 1992, pp. 117-33, for a description of the entire Prospective Principals Program curriculum at Stanford.

responsibility for it too big a deal in my own mind, I also limited my creativity in trying to help the group to be more creative and less stressed. . . . I find it difficult to fail, but no one died, and if I can learn about making mistakes and carrying on creatively despite them, particularly in not letting difficulties get me down, that will be progress. (Bridges with Hallinger 1992, pp. 78-79)

As participants' exposure to a PBL environment broadens and deepens, most become comfortable in working with adults and internalize the value of collaboration. An alumnus of the Stanford program captured these affective outcomes when she was asked to comment on the essays that students prepare following each project.

These essays give a sense of what students say and feel about their performance on specific projects. They are intentionally deeply reflective and thoughtful, and so do not convey the enthusiasm of people about this program and the PBL method. . . . The affective outcomes are not emphasized—the amazing camaraderie, the sensitivity to others, the change of intolerance to tolerance to acceptance to appreciation of different viewpoints— all these are important in the operational goal of the program, and in developing a new breed of administrator who won't settle for the isolation so characteristic of the principalship. (Bridges with Hallinger 1992, p. 68)

Content

Given that each project confronts students with multiple goals (that is, acquire problem-relevant knowledge, reach consensus on how to deal with the focal problem, and implement their solution), less content is covered in PBL than in conventional programs. Moreover, there is the ever-present danger that students will lose sight of the learning objectives and concentrate on solving the problem. Unless instructors take steps to ensure that students grapple with the content and how it applies to the focal problem, participants may overlook the learning resources that are provided.

Teacher

Faculty generally find PBL a satisfying way to teach. When describing their experiences with PBL, most highlight the students' level of motivation, the quality of their work, and their engagement with the classroom tasks. However, some instructors miss lecturing and become frustrated while watching their students grope and struggle with the messy realities of the problem. A few instructors express concerns about the interpersonal problems that sometimes arise in project teams and the "free rider" problem (letting other members do the work) that occurs when individuals are not held accountable.

In a PBL classroom environment that emphasizes doing, as well as knowing, some instructors make discomforting discoveries. By way of example, one professor wrote,

> The major discovery is how much I have learned as a professor about the quality of my instruction. The last group of students who solved a problem in my class were critiqued severely by a panel of superintendents. The students got defensive, but I realized that I did not prepare them well enough. . . . Students could write beautiful descriptions of how they would deal with problems... BUT THEY COULDN'T DO ANYTHING!!! Problem-based learning, especially with problems that require a reaction from a panel of experts, has caused me to look very carefully at my own teaching.

For other professors the discoveries are similarly enlightening but less painful. Two professors who experimented with our approach described their experiences as follows:

> Here was where we discovered one of the fundamental requirements of an effective PBL approach—the concept of "front-loading." We realized quite early that preparation for this course would mean a significant investment of time prior to the beginning of the class. . . . We discovered as soon as the class began how valuable front loading was. . . . We found that we were able to play different roles as instructors. Instead of believing we were obligated to "perform" each day in front of the class (and thereby convince ourselves that we were giving students their money's worth), we became more relaxed and under less pressure. Our role quickly evolved into one of a "coach," although we also had to be careful not to "over-coach" or "hover" as we called it. . . .

> In one of our post-class sessions one day, while discussing how the class had affected each of us, one of us termed the experience as transformative. By that he meant that he had come to see that with

adult learners especially, a much different approach was necessary. For years he had taught the same way that one would use to teach novitiates—that is, a heavy emphasis on content taught in a very didactic style. It became clear, however, in teaching this class that such an approach was inappropriate. (Chenoweth and Everhart 1994)

Conclusion

As we have argued in this opening chapter, PBL represents a bold, radical departure from the traditional way of preparing educational administrators. In our judgment, this approach can play an important, instrumental role in ensuring the success of educational reforms now under way. Administrators, like teachers, are being asked to move away from command-and-control models of leadership to "transformational" styles. Moreover, the kinds of teaching and learning advocated by reformers (teaching and learning for understanding) require administrators who act in ways consistent with these expectations and understand what active learning comprises. Problem-based learning holds promise for preparing the kind of leaders who can facilitate, rather than obstruct, these reforms.

Developing PBL Instructional Materials

Project development is more an art than a science.

W henever we discuss PBL with potential users, the conversation at some point turns to the issue of instructional materials. Eavesdropping on one of these conversations, we overhear the following:

> *Curious:* I've heard from others that PBL requires considerable upfront effort. Is that consistent with your (Ed's and Phil's) experience?

> *Ed:* Yes, PBL can involve a lot of front-loading, but there are ways to reduce it.

> *Curious:* Such as?

> *Phil:* We've found that the amount of time and effort users spend preparing for a PBL experience depends largely on three choices: (1) who develops the instructional materials for the project; (2) whether the user starts from scratch or adapts existing materials; and (3) what version of PBL one uses. Depending on your choices, you can spend anywhere from a few hours to a few weeks.

> *Curious:* I assume that starting from scratch to develop your own materials for a PBL project requires the most time. Is that right?

> *Phil:* Yes.

Curious: Since you have so much experience in developing PBL projects, I'd be interested in knowing how you proceed. I'm sure that I could reduce the front-loading if I didn't have to reinvent the process.

Ed: We'd like to think you could. If you have the time, we'll share with you what we have learned about the process of project development and the choices that affect how much front-loading of time and effort is involved.

Curious: Go ahead.

Major Choices in Project Development

We have discovered that three major choices determine the amount of time and effort that must be expended by the instructor when crafting projects for a PBL curriculum:

1. Who develops the project?

2. Should one start from scratch or adapt existing materials?

3. What version of PBL should be used?

Who Develops the Project?

We have used two different approaches to creating PBL projects. In the beginning, we developed our own materials and discovered that one project might take three weeks or more to create, field-test, and revise. As our familiarity with the process increased, we found that our time and effort decreased.

Later we used several formats to involve students in developing PBL projects. Some students have created and field-tested projects to fulfill the dissertation requirements for a Doctor of Education degree. Other students, working individually or cooperatively, have developed projects as part of a course. Irrespective of the format, students have found the challenge of developing a PBL project to be a satisfying, rewarding, and profoundly educational experience.

To facilitate project development by students, we provide them with a set of resources. Students first develop an understanding of PBL by reading material similar to that presented in chapter 1. In addition to this background material, students receive a copy of the template discussed in the next section, an example of a completed project, and a set of guidelines for using the template. These guidelines resemble the ones introduced following the detailed discussion of the template.

Prior to commencing the development of a project, we encourage students to submit a project prospectus. This prospectus requires students to describe their focal problem and its significance, the resources they anticipate needing to develop the project, a calendar for completing the various parts of their project, their preliminary thoughts about pilot-testing their work, and the biggest concerns or questions they have about their PBL project.

Our role during the development of the project is to provide feedback about the suitability of the project prospectus and to facilitate its completion by raising questions, suggesting possible resources, and commenting on the various components of their project.

Adapt Existing Materials or Start Anew?

Since PBL potentially requires considerable time and effort to implement, one can reduce the front-loading involved either by using materials developed elsewhere or by adapting existing materials, rather than starting from scratch. If one decides to use PBL on a trial basis, front-loading can be reduced substantially by choosing a project that is already available. Several projects appear in Appendix A and in the Appendix to *Problem-Based Learning for Administrators* (Bridges with Hallinger 1992). In addition, a series of PBL projects are also currently available through the ERIC Clearinghouse on Educational Management (ERIC/CEM). (See pages 193-94 for a list of titles and ordering information.)

The ERIC/CEM projects contain all the associated reading materials and can be purchased in multiple copies for students. A Teaching Note accompanies each of the ERIC/CEM projects. These Teaching Notes provide instructors with suggestions about how to use the projects most efficiently and effectively.

During the past few years, we have reduced our own front-loading by exchanging PBL projects with one another. In some instances, we have used the projects in their original form. In other instances, we have modified projects developed by others. Some project changes have been minor while others have been substantial.

For example, Hallinger and one of his students, Dr. Barbara Habschmidt, developed the *Something Old, Something New, and the Principal's Blues* project that is introduced later when we discuss the various components of a project. Bridges and one other professor have used this project; both have elected to substitute different readings but retained the rest of the project as it was originally developed. (This project, along with a Teaching Note, is available from ERIC/CEM under the title *Leadership and School Culture.*)

Bridges developed the *Write Right!* project (available with a Teaching Note from ERIC/CEM) for use in the Stanford Prospective Principals Program. Hallinger decided to use this project with a class of upperdivision undergraduates at Vanderbilt University. Given the nature of the group he was teaching and the purpose of the course, he retained the structure of the project but revised it substantially. His revisions included the following: minor changes in the Introduction, additional learning objectives emphasizing situational leadership, a new problem based on a case from the Harvard Business School series, a new set of guiding questions, revised product specifications, and some additional readings. Although these modifications were substantial, he saved considerable time by using the format and structure of the original project.

What Version of PBL?

As we noted in chapter 1, the basic unit of instruction in a problem-based learning curriculum is a project. These projects come in two forms: problem-stimulated and student-centered (Waterman, Akmajian, and Kearny 1991). The components of each project type are listed in table 2; in the next section, we discuss and illustrate each of these parts, while providing a template for their development.

TABLE 2		
Components of Problem-Stimulated and Student-Centered PBL Projects		
	Problem-Stimulated Projects	Student-Centered Projects
Features		
Introduction	x	x
Problem	x	x
Learning objectives	x	
Resources	x	
Product specifications	x	x
Guiding questions	x	
Assessment exercises	x	x
Time constraints	x	x

The major differences between the two types of projects center on who identifies the learning objectives, the resources, and the guiding questions. In problem-stimulated projects, the instructor assumes primary responsibility for identifying the learning objectives, the resources, and the guiding questions. In a student-centered project, the student assumes primary responsibility for these three components.

In terms of the front-loading involved, student-centered learning projects require less instructor time and effort. Since the students identify their own learning objectives, locate the relevant resources, and generate the guiding questions, the instructor does not need to spend time developing or updating these three components of a PBL project. Although less front-loading is required in creating a student-centered project, there are some costs. When given the opportunity to choose their own learning objectives, students may identify ones that only partially overlap with those objectives considered important to the faculty. Since students are generally less knowledgeable than faculty, they may fail to locate high-quality resources in the time available. Moreover, in student-centered projects, students may cover less of the content deemed desirable by the instructor than is possible in problem-stimulated projects.

Guidelines for Developing a PBL Project

When developing these guidelines, we assumed the following choices had been made: The instructor would create the project, the project would be started anew, and it would be problem-stimulated. These same guidelines can be used by students if the instructor chooses to involve them in developing a project.

The Template

As we indicated in the preceding section, each problem-stimulated project has eight major components: introduction, problem, learning objectives, resources, product specifications, guiding questions, assessment exercises, and time constraints. In the paragraphs that follow, we discuss each component and illustrate it by drawing from the project *Something Old, Something New, and the Principal's Blues* (Hallinger and Habschmidt 1994).

An Introduction

This component introduces the student to the focal problem for the project and provides a rationale for including the problem in the curriculum. The introduction states how and why the project is relevant to the work of the administrator and connects the problem and the learning objectives to the reality of the workplace.

SAMPLE INTRODUCTION

Projections of future trends in education indicate the need for an additional 200,000 public school teachers nationwide before the end of the twentieth century. These teachers will enter the work force in a societal context of increasing student enrollment and diversity, and rising expectations for instructional effectiveness. They will also comprise the first large cohort of beginning teachers to enter the profession after more than fifteen years of severely limited hiring.

Today teachers with twenty years or more of teaching experience comprise the largest portion of faculty members in most public schools. The percentage of teachers in the labor force who are aged forty-five years and older has increased dramatically since 1974. With a decade or more remaining in their careers, these individuals will continue to comprise the nucleus of the teaching staffs in most schools even as new teachers begin to enter the labor force during the 1990s. Thus, novice teachers will enter schools whose key participants are largely veteran teachers in the latter stages of their careers.

Principals will be faced with the challenge of managing the socialization of this cohort of new teachers in a fashion that promotes instructional effectiveness. The principal's success in meeting this challenge will be based in large part on his or her ability to reshape the culture of the school. Ideally, the new culture should meet the needs of both new and veteran teachers, as well as the desires of communities for quality instruction. Is that possible?

Problem

Each project is structured around a high-impact problem that the administrator is apt to face in the future. A high-impact problem is one that has the potential to affect large numbers of people for an extended period. Some of these problems are highly structured, while others are complex, messy, and ill-defined. These problems may take one of the following forms:

- *The swamp* (a complex mess containing numerous subproblems).

- *The dilemma* (The administrator knows what is wrong but is faced with choosing among alternatives involving a sacrifice or tradeoff of important personal and/or organizational objectives.)

- *The routine problem* (the type of problem that most administrators encounter annually, such as assigning teachers and students to various classes and courses).

- *The implementation problem* (The administrator is assigned a new policy or program to implement and must figure out how to ensure the successful implementation of this policy or program.) (Adapted from Bridges with Hallinger 1992, p. 96)

SAMPLE PROBLEM

It is now two months since you accepted the principalship at Unison Elementary School. As you ponder your accomplishments, you begin to feel rather blue. You inherited a veteran staff that the superintendent characterized as "dead in the water." In fact, the superintendent had made it clear that you were hired expressly because of his confidence in your ability to "get the beached whales moving again."

Although the superintendent had mentioned that the staff might have difficulty adjusting to a new principal, he had been crystal clear that his number one concern was the instructional effectiveness of the school. The primary reasons for the previous principal's early retirement were a three-year decline in the school's test scores and a growing perception that the school's faculty had "lost its edge." The staff had been very fond of the previous principal, John Larsen, who had led the school for the past twenty-five years. He had hired most of the teachers and was the only administrator for whom many had worked. They refer to him wistfully as a kind man who saw the world through rose-colored glasses. You have overheard staff members saying how much they miss his gentle way. One teacher stated that Unison School "would never be the same without him."

The Community

The demographics of this predominantly middle-class community had been stable for over twenty years. Two trends have been observed more recently, however. First, a large number of young parents have returned to the community so that their children could attend Unison as they did. These parents feel a strong commitment to Unison and are actively involved in a broad range of school activities through the Parent-Teachers Organization.

Second, over the past five years there has been a small but growing influx of immigrants into the community. These are the first students for whom English is not the primary language in the school district. These students appear eager to learn, but have experienced some adjustment problems in the regular instructional program offered by some of the teachers. When districtwide test results were discussed at the May meeting of the Board of Education, a few discontented parents from Unison complained that their children were not getting a first-rate education.

The Staff

One of the bright spots in your appointment had been the ability to hire three teachers this year to complement the four new teachers hired the previous year. On a faculty of twenty-five teachers, these were the first new hires in almost ten years. The only newcomers to Unison during that period were several transfers from other schools in the district, primarily to teach special education and ESL (English as a Second Language) classes.

The new hires represent an exciting resource for getting the school moving; however, they seem frustrated and unsure of themselves, despite their apparent talent and first-rate training. They appear to need more support in their classroom teaching as well as for their general professional well-being. You are similarly concerned with the dwindling enthusiasm of the four teachers hired last year.

The disturbing news doesn't end there, however. The veteran teachers seem angry and anxious. You sense a feeling of distrust. Your secretary has commented on more than one occasion that the "pillars" are having a hard time adjusting. She has heard them make comments like:

"Since when does the principal tell me how to teach."

"I suppose the district would like to see us get out of the way of these new teachers."

"Wait until the new people see how things really are!"

Something needs to be done before things get worse, but what?

[*Note*: Three appendices (omitted) provide additional information about the staff. Appendix A contains a table listing the names of staff members, along with their grade-level assignments, teaching experience, age, years at the school, and performance evaluations. Appendix B provides detailed profiles of ten teachers. Appendix C consists of a staff sociogram showing who interacts with whom.]

The Curricular and Instructional Program

Some years before, the district office had worked with a group of teachers from throughout the district to develop core curricular objectives for each grade level and subject area. Recommended materials and instructional methods were identified for each set of objectives. In the last three years, however, the district philosophy has changed. Individual schools are now allowed to choose curriculum materials and instructional programs (methods) to meet the core objectives. The strong emphasis placed on standardized test results still remains.

Teachers at Unison Elementary School have not responded to this change in philosophy. Only a few staff members are attempting new educational ventures. Three teachers are using a whole-language approach for teaching reading and writing. Two primary teachers, after attending a math workshop, are now trying a "hands-on" approach to teaching math with manipulatives.

The curriculum at Unison School reflects a traditional, back-to-basics approach. Many teachers rely on one textbook for each subject area taught. Although the previous principal purchased novels to support the whole-language approach to reading, the majority of the Unison staff continues to use a seven-year-old reading series. The two-year-old math textbook, selected by the staff, strongly emphasizes the use of manipulative materials at each grade level. You have noticed, however, that the manipulatives are stored in a closet in the teachers' lounge. As far as you can tell, nobody, other than the two primary teachers, have used them. Some of the materials still remain in the original packaging.

Teacher-directed instruction is prevalent in many of the classrooms. The thrust of student learning activities is on workbooks and ditto sheets. Students are ability-grouped at each grade level for reading and math. They change classes and teachers for instruction in these subjects. A few students are sent to a lower grade level to receive reading and math instruction.

Although severe discipline problems are infrequent, you have noticed more offtask behavior than you would like during your classroom visits. This is particularly apparent in the reading and math classes. You are also concerned by what appears to be a lack of participation by the ESL students in their regular classes.

Staff Development

The district office has traditionally been responsible for planning the professional growth and development activities for teachers. The district is considered generous and forward-thinking in its concern for staff development. Money for professional development is available through both the Human Resources and Curriculum and Instruction Departments, though Unison has not taken full advantage of this in the past. Teachers are expected to attend one annual institute designed and presented by the district office in August. Additional money is allocated for selected teachers in each building to attend conferences outside the district.

Teachers from Unison School have traditionally attended conferences on a rotating basis according to seniority. When you asked the assistant superintendent for instruction if this pattern of staff development could be changed, she replied, "It's seemed to work well in the past, though I guess that you could question some of the teachers' choices. You are free to make any proposal that can be justified. I'd be happy to look at whatever you put together."

Your Task

Your first-semester Building Status Meeting is scheduled for two weeks from today. You have been *warned* by fellow principals that these meetings are serious business. You have had two-and-a-half months to develop a plan for improvement. This is the meeting at which you must present it to the superintendent and his cabinet (assistant superintendents for curriculum and instruction, human resources, and business).

You are aware that the superintendent's priority is improving student achievement on standardized tests. You are also aware that he expects your plan to address the instructional effectiveness and revitalization of the Unison teachers. These meetings are treated as strategy sessions in which the superintendent's cabinet responds to the plan and the proposed strategy for implementation. The other principals have referred to these meetings as *shark* sessions—cabinet members being the sharks and principals the bait. To add more pressure to the situation, your colleagues remind you that this is a school board election year and the superintendent does not want any waves, only demonstrable improvement.

Learning Objectives

These objectives, limited in number, signal what knowledge and skills the student is expected to acquire during the project. These objectives emphasize higher order thinking skills (for example, evaluation and application), as well as knowledge acquisition.

SAMPLE LEARNING OBJECTIVES

By participating in this project, you will acquire knowledge and insight into how:

1. To implement major changes within a school setting

2. To develop a school culture that is conducive to personal and professional growth

3. To design a staff development program that:

   • is appropriate to the varied needs of adult learners

   • will promote faculty personal and professional growth

   • will improve teaching effectiveness

Resources

For each project, the student receives one or more of the following resources: books, articles, films, and consultants (professors or practicing administrators). The specific nature of the resources depends upon the learning objectives, the problem that is the focal point of the project, and the culminating product or performance. Since students often bring specialized knowledge and skills to a project, they should be encouraged to inventory the resources existing with their own project team and to exploit these resources. Moreover, they should be encouraged to take advantage of the material and human resources in their own districts and to use what they have learned in other courses.

SAMPLE RESOURCES

Videotape

"'Something Old, Something New, and the Principal's Blues': Perspectives from Theory, Research and Practice." (1 hr, 9 min)

[Two principals and two professors (Michael Fullan and Andrew Hargreaves) discuss their perspectives on dealing with this situation.]

Adult Development

Evans, R. "The Faculty in Midcareer: Implications for School Improvement." *Educational Leadership,* May 1989, pp. 10-15.

Krupp, J. "Understanding and Motivating Personnel in the Second Half of Life." *Journal of Education,* 169(1), 1987, pp. 20-46.

Staff Development

Sparks, D., and Loucks-Horsley, S. "Five Models of Staff Development for Teachers." *Journal of Staff Development,* 10, 4, 1989, pp. 40-57.

Joyce, B.; Showers, B.; and Rolheiser-Bennett, C. "Staff Development and Student Learning: A Synthesis of Research on Models of Teaching." *Educational Leadership,* October 1987, pp. 11-23.

Joyce, B., and Showers, B. "Improving Inservice Training: The Messages of Research." *Educational Leadership,* 37, 5 (February 1980), pp. 379-385.

School Culture

Deal, T., and Chatman, R. (1989). "Learning the Ropes Alone: Socializing New Teachers." *Action in Teacher Education,* XI, 1, pp. 21-29.

Robey, D. (1986). "Organizational Culture." In *Designing Organizations.* Homewood, Illinois: Irwin, pp. 436-455.

Saphier, J., and King, M. "Good Seeds Grow in Strong Cultures." *Educational Leadership,* March 1985, pp. 67-74.

Change

Fullan, M. (1991). "Planning, Doing, and Coping with Change." In *The New Meaning of Educational Change.* New York: Teachers College Press, pp. 94-113.

Fullan, M. (1991). "The Teacher." In *The New Meaning of Educational Change.* New York: Teachers College Press, pp. 117-143.

Principal's Role

Barth, R. (1981). "The Principal as Staff Developer." *Journal of Education,* Spring, pp. 144-163.

Leithwood, K. "The Principal's Role in Teacher Development." In *Changing School Culture Through Staff Development,* edited by B. Joyce. Alexandria, VA: Association for Supervision and Curriculum Development, 1990. Pp. 71-90.

McEvoy, B. (1987) . "Everyday Acts: How Principals Influence Development of Their Staffs." *Educational Leadership,* February 1987, pp. 73-77.

Programs for Recent Immigrants

Crossing the Schoolhouse Border. San Francisco: California Tomorrow.

Product Specifications

Each project culminates with some type of performance (for example, oral presentation), product (such as a memo), or both. In our experience, these culminating experiences, along with the focal problem, exert a profound influence on what students learn during the project. Therefore, it is imperative that the designers of the project choose their product or performance with considerable care. By varying the products (memo, presentation, conference, advisory groups, classroom observation report, and so forth), one can enhance the learning that occurs as a result of participating in numerous PBL projects.

These products ensure that students will be forced to deal with a host of issues involved in getting results through others. Team products require students to reach group decisions, to confront varying views about what the problem is and how it should be handled, and to figure out how they should organize themselves to create the product within the time constraints. These products provide a focus for the team's efforts, an incentive for learning, and a means by which the leader and team members can judge the effectiveness of their efforts.

Since real-world products are often ambiguous, the product specifications reflect similar levels of imprecision. Prospective administrators need to learn how to function effectively when the task is unclear and how to cope with the psychological discomfort that often accompanies such uncertainty.

SAMPLE PRODUCT SPECIFICATIONS

1. Prepare a three-year action plan (maximum of five pages) that reflects your solution to the problems at Unison School. Remember, you will be sharing this plan with the superintendent. Your plan should be a group product and should include the following sections:

    a. Definition of the problem as you view it at Unison; if you identify more than one problem, please prioritize those that you choose to address.

    b. A plan for addressing the important components of the problem; the plan should include sample activities, the sequence in which you intend to proceed with them, and your rationale for the selection and sequence.

    c. Your strategy for gaining the support of key actors and for overcoming the potential obstacles you will face implementing your plan.

This document should present the major dimensions of your plan for solving the problem at Unison Elementary School. Note, however, that the superintendent is interested in both formal and informal aspects of the strategy that you have developed for addressing the problem. He recognizes that plans must be adapted to various considerations, but is interested in seeing just what you have in mind for improving the problems in teaching and learning at Unison.

2. Prepare a fifteen-minute presentation to the superintendent's cabinet in which you describe your plan and discuss a solution to the

problems at Unison School. One member of the team will be selected by the instructor to give the presentation. The team will be responsible for assisting in the defense of its proposals.

Guiding Questions

With each project we provide several guiding questions. These questions serve several purposes: (1) to direct students to key concepts, (2) to assist students in thinking through the problem, and (3) to stimulate students to view the problem from alternative perspectives. Students may elect to discuss any of the questions that seem important to them or to ignore the questions completely. Accordingly, they are not required to prepare written answers to the guiding questions or to set aside time for discussing them. How students choose to use these questions rests entirely with them.

SAMPLE GUIDING QUESTIONS

1. What facets of the culture at Unison are likely to promote or impede change?

2. What are the potential leverage points for promoting change in this school's culture?

3. How do the motivation, commitment, and learning needs of adults at different ages and career stages influence the design of a staff development program? How do they influence the promotion of individual and schoolwide change?

4. What features of the school might shape the principal's introduction of change?

5. What role(s) should be considered for other stakeholders as the principal develops a strategy for change?

6. How will the audience influence the principal's presentation to the superintendent's cabinet?

Assessment Exercises

As we underscored in chapter 1, assessment in PBL serves learning and, thereby, promotes personal growth and improved performance. In line with this philosophy, assessment is used to accomplish several interrelated purposes:

- to revise projects to make them more productive and meaningful learning experiences for students

- to promote retention, transfer, and application

- to foster introspection and reflection

- to cultivate the appropriate use of knowledge and skills

These four purposes are accomplished in various ways. Throughout the project, students receive feedback regarding their process skills (for example, facilitating meetings, setting agendas, and handling conflict) and their utilization of the problem-relevant knowledge. At the conclusion of each project, students also receive feedback from a variety of sources about their final product and performance. In addition, each project contains assessment exercises that elicit students' reactions to the experience and stimulate them to reflect on what they have learned and how they might use these insights in the future.

SAMPLE ASSESSMENT EXERCISES

1. Prepare an essay (not to exceed two double-spaced, typewritten pages) that reflects what you have learned during this project and how the project might be modified to enhance your learning.

2. Complete the "Talk Back" sheet when you have finished the project.

Time Constraints

Most projects are designed to last from two to five sessions; each session is three hours long. Projects terminate when the learning and product objectives are achieved. The clock is a constant enemy in problem-based-learning projects. Team members find themselves continually struggling with the dilemma that confronts every conscientious manager, namely, how to achieve some reasonably high level of performance within severe time constraints. Managing this dilemma requires participants to make difficult choices and to set priorities (such as family vs. work, quantity vs. quality of output, and learning objectives vs. product objectives). Moreover, the dilemma underscores the need to work efficiently and to adopt time-saving measures.

SAMPLE TIME CONSTRAINTS

This project (Hallinger and Habschmidt 1994) has been used in a variety of settings—the Stanford University Prospective Principals Program, the Vanderbilt Principals' Institute, a PBL Institute for Professors, a two-week workshop for eighty principals, and a one-week workshop for principals. When we have used this project, we have usually allowed twelve to fifteen hours spread over a period ranging from two days to two weeks. Participants review the resources outside the time allotted for team meetings; in addition, participants often meet over breakfast, lunch, and dinner to work on their product.

Using the Template

To assist those who choose to use our template in developing a PBL project, we describe the process that we have generally followed. When reading our description, bear in mind that the actual process is less straightforward and sequential than our discussion suggests. The process is more fluid and dynamic; the developer moves back and forth among the components to ensure that they fit together to form a coherent role. Moreover, the process of project development is more challenging than it initially appears. In the words of one student,

> Developing the PBL project was far more work than I ever imagined. The project kept growing... I learned that although the projects look as though they'd be easy to develop when you're in class working on one; they aren't.

Although we organize our discussion of the process around each of the components, we have tried to show the relationships among a project's various parts. We have discovered that students often become preoccupied with getting the individual components right and lose sight of the linkages between and among them. One of our students underscored this point when he wrote in his "Talk Back":

> I learned the importance of integrating the introduction, learning objectives, performance requirements, resources and evaluation. I now view the project as more of a system than discrete parts. Seeing the interrelationship of the sections gave me new insights into the difficulty of developing a good PBL project and the power of that project for the participant.

The Problem

The starting point for developing a PBL project is a focal problem; the problem comes first, then the learning. When selecting a problem, the designer of the project should attempt to choose one that is representative of the kinds of problems students are likely to encounter in the roles and contexts for which they are being prepared. Moreover, the problem should be one with a high potential impact; that is, it affects large numbers of people for an extended period. Examples of such problems are the hiring of a new teacher, coping with the array of challenges inherent in a school undergoing transition from a homogeneous to a heterogeneous population, and implementing a controversial curricular change. (See Appendix B for tips on writing problem scenarios.)

Since an important skill to be obtained through problem-based learning is problem-finding, we strive to create problem scenarios that contain numerous subproblems. If the problems presented are too clearly defined, two things often happen. First, students lose the opportunity to engage in problem-finding. Second, the problem loses some of the flavor of reality. A large portion of the problems that administrators face are messy, ill-defined, and difficult to disentangle. Therefore, even if there is a set of technical skills that the designer wants students to acquire within a given project, it is likely that those skills will be used in an organizational setting that is rife with cultural norms, ethical conflicts, and corporate politics. Students need to experience applying technical skills with due consideration of the problematic contextual issues that tend to complicate organizational life.

Having chosen the problem to be included in the project, the developer then decides how to present it. Focal problems can be presented as a written case, a case incident (Pigors 1980), a live role

---

Features of Distinctive Problems

- High impact on the administrator, the organization, and/or clients
- Typical, rather than atypical, of administrator problems
- High importance to those experiencing it
- Messy, rather than narrow
- Realistic, not contrived
- Sufficient information for the reader to know what is in the situation and to prepare the products

---

play, a real-time issue, an interactive computer simulation, an interactive videodisc presentation, or a taped episode.

Sole reliance on written cases or verbal vignettes, as Bransford and others (1989) have noted, may have dysfunctional consequences for the learner. For example, the medical student who is trained to make a diagnosis based on verbal vignettes may be at a loss when confronted with real patients. Since the verbal vignette itself is "the output of an expert's pattern recognition process" (Bransford and others 1989, p. 484), the student may not learn "to recognize symptoms like 'slightly defensive' and 'moderately depressed' on their own."

To become an expert, a great deal of perceptual learning must occur, and this cannot happen unless the student learns to recognize the salient visual, auditory, and nonverbal cues. When designing a series of PBL projects, program designers should strive for a variety of modalities in presenting problems. If students encounter only verbal descriptions of problems, they may be unprepared to deal with real problems.

The Product

Once the problem and its mode of representation (for example, written case, case incident, or computer simulation) have been chosen, the next task is to specify the nature of the product or the performance that constitutes a resolution to the problem. The prod-

---

Features of Distinctive Products

- Forces students to go beyond analysis to actual implementation of the solution
- Mirrors the form and manner in which the administrator would resolve the problem in the real world
- Promotes collaboration among team members
- Builds on previous learning
- Requires a performance that is reasonable in light of the information provided about the problem and the context, the resources, the learning objectives, and the time allocated
- Identifies prerequisite skills needed for completing the product and provides the resources needed to acquire these skills

---

uct is the second most critical element of the project and shapes from the outset the students' perception of how the knowledge and skills to be acquired during the project figure into the work of a leader. Moreover, the product represents in the minds of students the action element of the project. The performance aspect of the product, therefore, acts as a major motivator and mediates the students' understanding of the project.

When creating products and product specifications, designers should strive to follow these guiding principles:

- Products should be authentic, that is, similar to the ones that an administrator would actually create or engage in when resolving the problem.

- Products by their very nature should enable students to use the knowledge and skills learned in this and previous projects (to the extent possible).

- Product specifications should require students to take action and to grapple with issues of implementation.

- Product specifications should place students in situations where they experience the consequences of their own actions and the actions of other team members. (Bridges with Hallinger 1992, p. 98)

If the project is one of a series, the following principles also apply:

- The form of the product (for example, memo and conference) should vary from one project to another to the extent possible.

- The product should require students to use basic skills learned in previous projects (for example, problem-solving, memo writing, and meeting management).

When developing the product specifications, we have found it useful to involve practicing administrators in designing realistic products and performances.

Learning Issues

With the focal problem and the culminating product or performance chosen, the next step is to identify the learning issues that are inherent in solving the problem and preparing the product. We have found it helpful in identifying the learning issues to distinguish between the problem-relevant knowledge that is the focus of the project and the related, requisite skills and knowledge that students need to complete the project successfully.

By way of illustration, let's revisit the project *In English, Please* that we discussed in chapter 1. As the reader may recall, this project centers on the various problems associated with serving a linguistically diverse student population. The culminating product involves preparing a set of materials for the first meeting of the Bilingual Advisory Committee. When generating the potential learning issues, we first focused on the problem-relevant knowledge by convening a group of relevant experts and asking them the same sorts of questions that we ordinarily pose to ourselves:

- What knowledge (theory and research) is most directly pertinent to the core issue in the problematic situation? [bilingual education and second-language acquisition]

- What other knowledge (for example, legal, financial, historical, organizational, political, and psychological) might be helpful to the student in understanding and dealing with this situation? [historical—treatment of language minorities in the United States; and legal—state and federal laws and guidelines for programs serving limited-English-proficient students]

Once we identified the problem-relevant knowledge, we turned to uncovering the additional skills and knowledge required to complete the project. These skills and knowledge are more difficult to discern because they are often implicit and taken for granted. In an effort to identify these potential learning issues, we considered such skills as the following: problem-solving, running meetings, managing task forces, preparing memos, making oral presentations, and conducting conferences. If we suspect that students may lack one or more of these skills, we include them in our list of learning issues. In this instance, we identified managing an advisory committee or task force as an important requisite skill and a potential learning issue on the grounds that most students would likely lack this skill.

Learning Objectives and Resources

Describing the focal problem, specifying the product or performance, and identifying the potential learning issues lay the groundwork for choosing the major learning objectives and the key resources. In selecting these major objectives, we generally emphasize ones that relate to the learning issues identified as directly relevant to the core issue in the problematic situation. When constructing these objectives, we strive to state them in terms of what students are expected to learn from the project, not in terms of what they will be doing in the project.

The resources that we include with each project cover a broader range of learning issues than the ones directly applicable to the learning objectives. In addition, these resources illuminate various facets of the problematic situation (for example, pertinent legal and historical content), and they provide knowledge and skills that students may lack but are essential to solving the problem and/or preparing the product. Whenever possible, the resources expose students to the relevant theory and research and provide examples of how the theory and research have been translated into educational policy and practice.

Features of Distinctive Learning Objectives

- Stress different learning domains (that is, cognitive, skill, and affective)
- Emphasize development of comprehension, analysis, application, and synthesis, as well as knowledge
- Appear reasonable in scope given the other parts of the project (for example, time constraints, resources, problem, and product)
- Accent what students will learn from the project, not what they will be doing to prepare the product

---

In choosing resources for a project, we have used consultants in various ways. For example, practitioners who have encountered similar problems in their own professional practice may be invited to suggest materials that they have found useful in understanding and dealing with the problem that is the focal point of the project. Practitioners and professors who are expert in the problem may also be provided for the students as they work on the project.

When we include consultants, we establish a set of norms. Consultants are prohibited from providing advice on how to handle the problem. Instead, they are encouraged to answer questions that

---

Features of Distinctive Resources

- Variety of forms (print, video, human, and so forth)
- Useful in framing/resolving the problem and developing the product
- Interdisciplinary, rather than single subject
- Representative of the types of knowledge (theory, research, practical wisdom) and points of view relevant to the problem
- Reasonable number in light of time constraints

---

students might raise in relation to the problem and to raise questions that might sensitize students to aspects of the problem they may have overlooked.

Guiding Questions

The next step in the process of developing a PBL project involves stating a set of "guiding questions." When we discussed the template in an earlier section, we suggested three purposes that may be served by these questions. In choosing which purposes to emphasize, we generally have relied on our judgment about whether the problem was so messy and complex that students may need some assistance in thinking through the problem. We also have considered whether students are likely to frame the problem by making a fundamental error, namely, viewing the problem solely from the perspective of the people involved. Finally, we have exercised our judgment as to whether students may overlook or dismiss without much thought concepts that may prove useful in illuminating and dealing with this type of problem.

Features of Distinctive Guiding Questions

- Stimulates consideration of alternative viewpoints
- Suggests issues that may not be apparent to students given their stage of professional development
- Foreshadows issues that pertain to the product, as well as to the problem
- Raises issues relevant to the knowledge domains included in the resources

---

Assessment Exercises

With each project, we include several types of assessment exercises in service of learning. To ensure that projects continue to provide productive and meaningful learning experiences, we include a "Talk Back" sheet (see last page of Appendix A). At the completion of a project, students use the "Talk Back" sheet to discuss what they liked about the project and how it might be improved. Their suggestions for improvement usually center on the resources, the problem, or the product. Regardless of how many times the project has been used, we continue to solicit students' reactions to it. Through repeated assessments conducted over time, we can obtain suggestions for improving the project and determine when it no longer provides a productive and meaningful learning experience for students.

To encourage reflection, retention, and transfer, we ask each student to prepare a two-page integrative essay at the end of each project (see chapter 4 and Bridges with Hallinger 1992, pp. 65-87, for numerous examples). These essays capture what students have learned and how they propose to use their knowledge in the future. The designer of the project should suggest some possible questions for students to address in this essay. We have suggested questions like the following:

- What principles or approaches have you learned in working with this problem that will help as you work on future problems with similar characteristics?

- What new information did you acquire that changed your knowledge and understanding of this problem?

- Is it possible for you to construct an outline, model, or generalization about the processes involved in dealing with this problem?

- What have you learned about project leadership, meeting management, problem-solving, and the work of the principal that may be of use to you in the future?

- What did you learn about yourself, your ability as a leader, and your participation in a management team as you worked on this project?

- What did you learn in a previous project that proved helpful in this one or needed to be revised in light of what happened during this project?

- What strongly held personal views, beliefs, or opinions have been changed during this project?

- What questions have been raised in working with this problem that suggest the need for further study? (Bridges with Hallinger 1992, pp. 66-67)

Depending on the preferences of the designer, the student may be given the option of choosing what to discuss from a list of possible questions or may be required to discuss one or two questions of particular interest to the person constructing the guidelines for the essay.

If the problem-relevant knowledge is relatively technical (for example, the legal requirements for particular programs like special education), the designer may wish to include a knowledge-review exercise and to provide the answer key after students complete the exercise. In the chapter on student assessment, we supply an example of a knowledge-review exercise.

Time Constraints

Setting realistic time limits for a project becomes more feasible as the designer gains experience with PBL. In the beginning, one can expect to underestimate the time students need to complete a project. The upside of underestimating the time is that it provides students with an opportunity to experience how they react to the stress and time pressures that are so characteristic of managerial work. However, the downside is that underestimates can frustrate students and result in their slighting the learning to "get the product out the door." Given this potentially undesirable outcome, we are now inclined to make liberal estimates of the time required to acquire the knowledge and to use it to produce a high-quality product or performance. If students lack a background in meeting and project management and have not worked together previously, they will require even more time to complete a project.

Introduction

Although this component of a project appears first, we have discovered that it is easier to prepare the "Introduction" last. Possessing greater familiarity with the problem, the product, the learning objectives, and the resources, one has a deeper sense of how and why the project is relevant to the work of the administrator.

When writing the "Introduction," different techniques can be used to engage the reader. An interesting quote or an anecdote can capture the readers' interest and assist them in understanding why the problem to be addressed in the project is important. Citing statistics that show the prevalence of the problem in schools can also underscore the significance of the problem. For example, in the project *In English, Please,* we call attention to the large and growing number of limited-and-non-English-proficient students in the public schools and the challenges that the schools face in dealing effectively with this population.

Identifying the consequences of failing to handle the problem successfully can further highlight its importance and relevance. For example, choosing the wrong candidate for a teaching position creates numerous future problems—time spent on responding to student and parent complaints, assisting the teacher, and documenting the teacher's poor performance; diminished educational opportunities for students; and profound pain and anguish for the teacher and administrator if the teacher must be dismissed.

Features of Distinctive Introductions

Content
- Describes how and in what form this issue arises in the current educational context
- Indicates why this issue is salient to administrators
- Suggests how the knowledge and skills included in the project are useful in dealing with this issue

Style
- Engages the reader
- Uses active voice and straightforward, intelligible language
- Discusses the content succinctly and to the point

Finally, concluding the introduction with a statement that tells readers explicitly what they are going to learn through this project may stimulate their interest in the project.

Field-Testing the Project

When the designer has completed a draft of the project, it should be field-tested. The importance of field-testing a project is reflected in this student's comments:

> The field test was essential. I thought the project was in good shape, but the test revealed it needs more depth and more clarity in the instructions.

We heartily agree with her observation; other project developers have echoed these same sentiments.

Prior to the main field-test, we have found it useful to conduct a preliminary field-test. This dry run ordinarily occurs with a small group of colleagues (students or faculty) whom we have asked to review the project and to provide feedback. Their feedback usually centers on the clarity and unity of the project, as well as the suitability of the resources and the guiding questions. Their comments often lead to another round of revision prior to the main field-test.

The main field-test represents the real thing. Students receive a copy of the entire project (all components), along with the resources, and implement it within the time constraints. By observing students work on the project and reviewing their "Talk Back" sheets, the author of the project may discover problems like the ones that we have uncovered in our own field-tests. The following are representative of issues that we have encountered:

- Students experienced the problem or the product as contrived.

- We overlooked some critical knowledge or skills students needed to complete the project successfully.

- The instructions or guidelines that we gave the persons providing the feedback were inadequate.

- We either underestimated or overestimated the time required to complete the project.

- We included too many resources.

- Some of our resources were either poorly written or of little value in dealing with the problem or preparing the product.

- Our guidelines for the product were too ambiguous.

- The various components of the project were insufficiently linked.

When issues like these surface during the main field-test (as they nearly always do), they become an occasion for revising the project.

Conclusion

Developing PBL projects and instructional materials is a formative, iterative, and continuous process. The process relies heavily on student feedback gathered in a systematic fashion each time the project is used. This developmental process comes to an end only when the project becomes outdated and no longer serves the purposes for which it was created. Before that time arrives, the author of the project and the students who have participated in it will have savored the joy, the satisfaction, and the challenge inherent in problem-based learning. In our experience, the front-loading inherent in PBL is worth it.

3

Implementing Problem-Based
Learning in the Classroom

We recently conducted a training program for staff developers who had been charged with using problem-based learning in a professional-development institute for urban principals. On the first morning, the participants engaged in an actual problem-based-learning project, *Because Wisdom Cannot Be Told*. The objectives of this PBL project are that students learn what problem-based learning is, the rationale behind it, and how it operates in the classroom.

During the classroom session, participants sought to achieve these objectives through solving a realistic problem. They worked in small groups, largely independent of the instructor, using a set of relevant text and video resources on PBL. The project culminated with each group delivering a report that outlined its proposed resolution of the problem presented in the project (see Appendix A).

In the debriefing that followed, one participant commented on the instructor's classroom role during the PBL project.

> I know you were doing a lot during the actual PBL session, even though it wasn't necessarily obvious to us. In thinking back, I recall that you sat in on my group periodically, but made only a few comments. You interrupted the large group a couple of times for announcements but this was pretty minimal given that we worked in our teams for four hours.

Still, I'm sure you were actually doing many things that facilitated our ability to learn so much in such a short period of time. Much of your own decisionmaking as the teacher, however, was hidden from our view. What were you were thinking and doing, both before and during the project in your role as the teacher? We need to understand this if we're going to use PBL successfully in our own institute.

On the one hand, it was refreshing to hear a potentially critical audience draw the conclusion that the teacher's inactivity during the PBL project was only an illusion! On the other hand, his query forced us to stop and reconsider, "What were we doing that someone would need to know to use problem-based learning in the classroom?"

In this chapter we explore key facets of the instructor's role in implementing PBL in a classroom setting. Before beginning, we must reiterate how the form of PBL that we use differs from the approaches commonly used in problem-based medical education. The differences may not appear large, but they have a significant impact on many aspects of classroom implementation.

Comparison with PBL in Medical Education

Problem-based medical education uses a *tutorial* format in which students work in groups to solve an assigned problem. A *tutor*, usually a professor or advanced graduate student, facilitates the process by which students engage the problem. The tutor also provides occasional clarification of knowledge issues that arise. Thus, in a medical-education setting the PBL tutor does not provide direct instruction, but he or she does remain an active facilitator and central figure in the group's learning process (for example, see Barrows and Tamblyn 1980, Neame 1989, Nova n.d., Walton and Matthews 1989, Wilkerson and Hundert 1991).

In problem-based leadership education, students also work in cooperative groups. However, two essential characteristics of the group-learning process distinguish this model from the medical-education model. First, students work without the facilitation of a faculty tutor. They manage virtually the entire process of their learning for the full duration of each PBL project.

In designing PBL for leadership education, we chose this format because we believe that an essential element of effective leadership is the capacity to achieve results through people. The actual classroom process in problem-based leadership education, therefore, emphasizes the development of skills that enable administrators to achieve this end. As managers of their own team learning process, students must learn and practice skills in meeting management, time management, conflict resolution, and group problem-solving and decision-making.

Understandably, medical educators view the development of these capacities as secondary to the learning goals for future doctors. Consequently, they see less to be gained through ceding full control over the learning process to students. They also give less explicit attention to the development of these skills as goals of the curriculum.

Second, our PBL model places a greater emphasis on the implementation of actions that lead toward the resolution of problematic situations. Problem-based medical educators give greater weight to understanding the scientific and human processes that underlie medical problems than to the resolution of the problem. Since both problem-analysis and implementation skills are essential to effective leadership, we explicitly incorporate action-oriented performances into our PBL projects. The demand for an active resolution of the problem offers students the opportunity to experience, even in a limited fashion, the consequences of their analytical plans as well as to practice skills they will need in the workplace (for example, conferencing, memo writing).

We note these differences because they have far-reaching and quite specific implications for the roles of the instructor and students in our model of PBL. In a previous volume, we provided an indepth view of what PBL looks like in the classroom and briefly discussed the role of the instructor (see chapters 3 and 4, Bridges with Hallinger 1992). In this chapter we extend the earlier discussions by providing a detailed answer to the question posed by the staff developer in our PBL training program: *What were you thinking and doing, both before and during the project, in your role as the teacher?*

We begin by discussing some of the attitudes of the instructor that appear to characterize successful implementation of PBL. Then we explore issues that arise before, during, and after the implementation of a PBL unit of instruction (that is, the learning project).

Faculty Attitudes for Success in a Problem-Based-Learning Environment

In feedback following an undergraduate leadership-education course that used PBL extensively, students used several metaphors to describe the teacher's role, including "guide," "resource," and "lighthouse." These metaphors highlight the relative inactivity of the teacher when compared with either a traditional teaching role or with the activities of students during a PBL project. As a lighthouse, "the teacher periodically casts a beam towards the field of activity, illuminating potentially lethal hazards, but leaving all discussion of alternatives and decisions to act in the hands of the travellers."

This shift for the teacher requires considerable attention by the instructor to both affective and cognitive dimensions of the role. Prior to discussing what we do in the classroom, we wish to note some attitudes of the instructor that contribute to a healthy problem-based-learning environment. These attitudes shape the teacher's behavior and, in a sense, represent prerequisites for successful problem-based instruction.

Confidence in the PBL Process

While the statement may appear self-evident, we begin by asserting that the instructor must be confident PBL can result in the desired types of learning. The learning environment experienced by students in PBL is so different from the norm that misgivings on the instructor's part tend to magnify students' natural apprehensions. It is predictable that, at some point during a PBL project, students will feel like ships lost at sea. Particularly at these moments, the instructor must maintain confidence that the PBL process can work. Melinda Hall, a Vanderbilt doctoral student who observed and analyzed the process of a PBL class, captured this unfolding process:

[Early in the term] students expressed considerable confusion. . . . mixed with nervousness about the "hands-off" approach of the professor, the lack of direction, the ambiguity of the class. . . . As the semester continued, however, they not only began experiencing less confusion but they also referred back in a distinctly positive light to the confusion they had formerly expressed in negative terms. . . . [W]ith hindsight they saw the value of experiencing the PBL modules through a "baptism by fire" and a "you're on the ice" method. . . .

One student noted that as the course progressed she began to look forward to succeeding modules and the process that she understood would unfold. She said that she had come to realize that the ambiguity inherent both in the problems presented in the learning module and in the process of group formation at the beginning of each project would be resolved by the team. This knowledge gave her confidence in herself and her peers. Responding successfully to the challenges that accompany the PBL process resulted in a great deal of personal satisfaction. (Hall 1994, p. 5)

In a sense, the instructor must maintain a vantage point above the affective and cognitive turmoil that students experience during the classroom process of PBL. From atop the lighthouse, the teacher needs to preserve the perspective that for the students being *lost at sea* is part of the journey; not far off, near the horizon, are calmer waters that lead toward the desired destination.

This attitude not only allows the instructor to convey confidence to students, but it also shapes the subsequent actions that he or she takes to support their learning. As we discuss later in the chapter, it also enables the instructor to avoid unnecessary actions in response to the students' confusion.

Experimentation

A principal we know displays this slogan on his desk: "Anything worth doing is worth doing poorly." This reversal of the common adage often causes his visitors to ask, "Why on earth would you want to provide that as a model for your students and faculty?" He usually responds:

It's been my observation that the greatest impediment to trying something new for students, and even more for my veteran faculty, is the fear of failure. Yet, virtually all of our real learning involves risk-taking. I want my staff and students to know that I support the possibility of their short-term failure in the longer-term goal of their learning. (Beaty 1987)

A similar attitude serves an instructor well in a PBL environment. We have already noted that in PBL the instructor must be confident in the problem-based-learning process. At the same time, however, he or she must also maintain an open-minded attitude about how that learning process may unfold. In regard to both *what* and *how* students are learning, the teacher must be prepared to support students' self-directed efforts at learning.

The problem-stimulated version of PBL that we discuss in this book offers students a set of desired learning objectives. The instructor should, however, also encourage students to use PBL projects as vehicles for working toward their own personal learning objectives. At times this takes individual students in some unanticipated directions. This may result in detours from the instructor's intended learning. We believe, however, that the benefits of supporting students' experimentation and decision-making outweigh the costs.

Consequently, a well-designed PBL project rarely turns out the same way twice! Even two groups working on the same project at the same time may emerge with quite different interpretations of the problem as well as with products that incorporate contrasting solutions. Rather than press for uniformity, we encourage alternative approaches to the problem.

For example, the project *Something Old, Something New, and the Principals' Blues* (published by ERIC/CEM under the title *Leadership and School Culture,* Hallinger and Habschmidt 1994) addresses how a principal can initiate improvement in a school with a stagnating culture that resists change. Recently the school received an infusion of enthusiastic but young and inexperienced teachers. Its students increasingly come from culturally diverse homes quite different from the traditional population of the school. Thus, change—though unwanted—is beginning to permeate the school both inside and outside.

In a professional-development institute at Vanderbilt University, two groups of principals viewed this same situation from contrasting perspectives. One team interpreted the problems presented in this project in terms of the discontinuity between the school and its changing community. Their analysis led to a solution that celebrated multiculturalism within the school community. They used this theme as an action vehicle for stimulating change in curriculum and teaching.

A second group of principals, for whom multicultural issues were less personally salient, viewed the problem primarily in terms of its technical subsystems. Their solution focused on curriculum alignment and staff development designed to bring about more effective teaching. These two directions, as different as they were, reflected reasonable approaches to the problem, particularly given the assumptions about the school that were stated by the groups. The differences in interpretation and action vehicles for change became occasions for additional learning for the students from both groups.

An attitude of experimentation must also characterize the instructor's approach to the project materials. While it may seem obvious that the first-time use of a PBL project involves considerable experimentation, we approach each PBL unit as if it's in a process of continuous development. We believe that no PBL project is a *finished product*. Even with projects that have been used on numerous occasions, we see opportunities for modifications, particularly in the learning objectives, resources, and product specifications. Thus, in these respects we believe that an attitude of experimentation on the teacher's part leads to instructional behaviors that support problem-based learning.

Patience

In hand with experimentation is a need for the instructor to develop patience. As we have indicated, the process of PBL involves trial and error and a large dose of student-directed learning. At times this may seem inefficient. However, instructors must cultivate patience to let students assume responsibility and ownership for the process and products of their learning.

We afford students considerable responsibility and latitude in how they carry out the learning process within a given learning project. Not surprisingly, the manner in which students engage themselves in a project varies widely. This can strain the instructor's needs for a smooth, predictable journey during the project.

For example, we ask our students to learn and use the Interaction Method of meeting management (Doyle and Straus 1976) as a tool for group work. This is generally introduced in an initial project. Then students are encouraged, though not required, to practice this structured method of meeting management over the course of subsequent projects.

Typically, however, a time comes during the course of a term when the groups are running smoothly and students no longer feel the need for the structured roles indicated in the Interaction Method. They often decide—sometimes explicitly or more often implicitly—to "just work as a group." Predictably, when this occurs, the groups also begin to experience all the problems that arise in groups in the absence of a means of managing the group's work process.

As an instructor, it is often painful to watch the group at this stage when it seemingly takes several steps backward. While an admonition or comment from the instructor could seemingly save time and set the group back on the right track by telling them what to do, most groups find their way back onto the track through their own self-assessment and problem-solving. In fact, we find that our attempts to shortcut the learning process through such interventions often end up leading students on detours that are less productive than if we let them work through problems on their own. The benefits are far greater when the students make the decision—which has been the case with virtually all groups with whom we have worked—to go back to the structure of the Interaction Method of their own accord. They subsequently work with intimate knowledge of the experience of the consequences of working under two different modes of operation. This was observed in one of our PBL classes.

> [Over the course of the term] as students worked more in teams, the [meeting management] roles became both more clearly defined and valued. The leaders began to provide more detailed agendas and introduced them with phrases such as, "I hope this will provide a plan to keep us focused." Facilitators took more initiative to. . . provide the direction so that other members could concentrate on the content of discussions rather than on the process. Finally, group members began to take it upon themselves to challenge each other, with some groups assigning "devil's advocates" in order to become more critical in their evaluation of possibilities under discussion. (Hall 1994, p. 6)

While it has been a challenge to cultivate the necessary self-discipline after careers of telling or leading students to see important issues and concepts, patience does have its rewards for the instructor. First, patience allows the instructor to sit and listen to the thinking that goes on as students struggle to understand and to apply concepts to real problems. While at times this is frustrating, on the whole it is invigorating to watch the students' learning unfold and, perhaps for the first time, really hear how students are interpreting theories, research, and problems.

In addition, students report that this type of learning experience is worthwhile. Through their integrative essays as well as their other learning products, we are able to see development in salient knowledge, skills, and attitudes. Cognitive theory indicates that this type of learning process fosters retention after students leave the classroom. These seem like worthwhile benefits from the perspective of the instructor.

Supportiveness

The PBL classroom environment places not only the instructor but also students in a situation of substantial challenge and risk-taking. The manner in which students experience this change was captured in an integrative essay written by an undergraduate student at Vanderbilt University following the PBL project *Making Change for School Improvement*. In this essay, reproduced below, the student draws a salient parallel between the reactions of school people to change in a PBL project on change implementation and the process of personal change that she experienced as she sought to adapt to the PBL classroom environment.

STUDENT RESPONSE TO THE PBL CLASSROOM ENVIRONMENT

After we had completed the change module, I realized that I had gone through these same stages during this course. At the start of the semester, I didn't know anything about PBL; experiencing this in class was new and different. . . . At first I was turned off by the concept because I didn't know anything about it. Like the people in the school district in the PBL project, I didn't see a need to change the way classes were being taught. . . .

After I was given the materials on PBL, it seemed like an interesting concept, but I was still resistant towards the change, mostly because it was new. I was unfamiliar with the teaching procedure, the grading criteria, the role of the student, and the role of the teacher. Again, like [the people in] the school district, I was intimidated by the change. At this point in the course we started immediately working on a PBL project and it took some of the mystery away about the new curriculum and reduced the intimidation. . . .

I soon found myself asking my friends and advisor what they thought about the PBL method. I was very much influenced by what the people in my social circle had to say (I know this is not always a good quality, but it's what happened). We also saw this happen in the school district in the project where certain informal leaders influenced [the opinions and attitudes of] others in their social circles. . . . We were able to *move* people like myself who were slower to change once we talked with and got the support of these informal leaders. . . .

As the semester progressed, I found that it was increasingly difficult to remain resistant! The class was moving along and we were getting more and more involved in our PBL projects. Working in groups and solving real problems was seeming more like a challenge than a chore. Using the PBL method began to get easier and more comfortable. This, in particular, relates to applying the Interaction Method to our group meetings. We saw this change with most of the teachers and administrators during the PBL project as well. The more they were exposed to the curriculum and supported it through practice, the easier it became to use it. Eventually, where we were successful as facilitators of the change process, more of the school staffs routinely used the new curriculum, even when it wasn't being required or monitored.

As this student's insight indicates, the PBL learning environment poses a challenge for students who are accustomed to more traditional forms of instruction (also see the videotape, *Can We Make a Better Doctor?*). One way to build confidence in the method — for both the instructor and students — is through the systematic introduction of PBL to students. We take several steps to support students' transition to a PBL environment.

When PBL is used in conjunction with university courses, we facilitate transition first through the syllabus (see sample "Class Schedule" in Appendix C, pages 178-79) and then through direct engagement in the specially designed introductory PBL project contained in Appendix A. The syllabus describes in some detail the expectations of the instructor, the nature of the instructional methodology, and the role of the student in PBL. This alerts students that a change is in the offing.

At the outset of the course, we have students complete the project *Because Wisdom Cannot Be Told*. As noted earlier, this short (four- to five-hour) project was designed as a means of informing students about PBL and how it operates in the classroom (see Appendix A). Feedback from students indicates that this immediate, first-hand experience of PBL, though initially intimidating, is a helpful vehicle for preparing them to make the transition to PBL. Students' "Talk Back" sheets frequently note how initially they didn't see how it would be possible to accomplish the product specifications for this project within the time allotted. Yet they also note surprise, pride, and satisfaction at finishing the project with demonstrably higher levels of knowledge, skill, and confidence concerning PBL. This early success fosters students' confidence in the instructor, the PBL method, and their capacity to work in a student-directed learning environment.

Although it is not always possible to do so in a professional-development setting, within the university context we also try to support student success in PBL by using a staged approach in the curriculum. That is, at the earlier stages of student's exposure to PBL, we select PBL projects that are less complex in terms of the number and "swampiness" of the problems they present. We consciously sequence projects, gradually increasing the prerequisite skills and knowledge (for example, meeting management, problem-solving, oral and written presentation) that the projects demand of students.

Given the dramatic shift in the norms within a PBL environment, it is important that the instructor support student efforts whether or not they initially succeed. As we have already noted several times, we do this by letting them work through the problems they encounter with only limited intervention on our part. By doing so, we communicate our confidence in their ability to succeed. Of course, we also make ourselves, as well as other human resources, available during the project. We do not let them feel abandoned.

As one of our students observed of the professor, "He let us do it, and made us think more, and because we had to think more, we learned more in retrospect." Another noted that the instructor "wanted us to discover and be comfortable learning on our own. That was very good for me. . . . If we were getting off track *too* far he would guide us, and when we had questions he would answer us, so we knew the support was there from him."

We also provide support for students by building a system of extensive, ongoing formative feedback throughout the course of a PBL project. We cannot overemphasize the importance of feedback for students in a PBL environment. As Hall notes, the instructor "expected [students] to encounter frustration, but then to learn from it. The constructive nature and detail of [the instructor's] feedback 'floored', 'baffled', and 'astonished' them. They . . . valued it, especially as they saw the benefits unfolding throughout the year" (1994, p. 12).

Feedback on student efforts is conveyed through periodic, oral peer assessments in each of the groups during the project, an instructor-led oral debriefing with the whole class following completion of a project, written feedback concerning the products (at times individually to students and always to the groups) at the end of a project, and conversations with individual students during the project. We elaborate on issues of feedback in the final section of this chapter and also in the chapter on student assessment. Here we simply note that nonjudgmental, specific feedback to students on their thinking, behaviors, and work products represents a powerful and essential form of support.

High Expectations

The last of the attitudes we wish to highlight is high expectations for student success. The emphasis that we place on experimentation, supportiveness, formative assessment, and self-directed learning by no means diminishes our expectations concerning student effort or our standards for accomplishment of learning objectives. High expectations for students are critical within a PBL environment since the instructor is, in a sense, seeking to replace traditional classroom-control mechanisms with group norms and self-motivation as motivators of student effort.

Our experience with PBL in a variety of settings and with a wide range of students bears out the belief that students apply themselves with greater effort and more time to the tasks within problem-based learning than in traditional instruction. Similar reports have emerged in the medical-education literature. This has even been cited by some as a potential drawback on the grounds that PBL demands too much of students (Parks 1994).

We find this concern ironic in that educational administration is a field in which students typically attend graduate programs on "tired time" after work or on weekends. The negative consequences for learning standards and expectations that arise from these conditions of graduate study have been discussed at length (Bridges 1977, Hallinger and Murphy 1991, Murphy 1993). If it is true that some students experience PBL as overly intense and taxing, we believe it worthwhile to err on the side of demanding too much rather than too little of our students. In fact, our students report consistently that while they find PBL demanding, the benefits for their learning are worth the effort. At the same time, the reader should know that in neither of our university programs in educational administration does problem-based learning represent the only instructional strategy in use.

We seek to communicate high expectations for student success in a variety of ways. Foremost among these is giving students responsibility for managing their own learning during the course of a PBL project. As noted earlier, this includes planning and managing the steps for project completion, how they will use the time allocated for the project, the process and content of meetings, and the learning resources. Giving control for these aspects of the class over to students has had some unanticipated and surprisingly positive consequences.

We find that when given control over how to use their time, students invariably spend more rather than less time on their work. For example, in a weekend class of veteran urban administrators in the Vanderbilt doctoral program, the students engaged the instructor in the classic struggle to reduce class time when using teacher-directed instruction (in this instance, simulations). When the class switched into a PBL mode, the teacher gave students full control over use of the time allocated for the project (in this instance, twelve hours of class time). The result was that the students stayed in class longer than had been scheduled by the instructor during the previous weeks (that is, when the students sought to negotiate less class time)!

When queried as to why they had chosen to work longer when they now had the freedom to come or go as they pleased, a veteran elementary school principal replied: "Isn't that human nature. When you give people the responsibility for their own circumstances they usually exceed what you would expect of them if you maintained the control yourself." We have observed a similar phenomenon with undergraduate students who actually set up extra team meetings on dates when class was cancelled.

Similarly, when students are given control over *how* they learn, we also find that they exceed our normally high expectations. When students are provided with a set of resources that are relevant to understanding and solving a problem perceived as meaningful, they consistently make use of them. At Vanderbilt in an undergraduate course on organizational change, one of our students noted this tendency in an integrative essay:

> Most professors here would be satisfied if 70% of their students came to class and had read 70% of the materials. It has been my experience in this class that virtually 100% of the students have come to this class each week, and that to a person they have actually done all of the readings designated by the group. . . your group forces you to pull your own weight.

We have had similar experiences in less mainstream settings. Recently one of us was planning a week-long institute for principals in Kentucky. The program's coordinator heard that we were planning for the participants to work independently in groups each afternoon during the institute. She shared her concern:

> You know, these folks are not Vanderbilt or Stanford doctoral students. What will we do if they just go home each day at 1:00 p.m. after you release them to their teams? And you know, they're not used to doing much, if any, professional reading. What if they just skip over the entire notebook of readings and resources?

While these concerns were legitimate and reflected prevailing norms in many professional preparation and development programs, after further discussion we agreed to set high expectations. Consistent with our prior experiences in PBL, the participants exceeded our expectations. Like the doctoral students, they set up breakfast and lunch meetings for their groups and stayed longer than designated by the program each day. Analysis of their work products and periodic observations of their meetings also clearly demonstrated that time, effort, and attention had been given to a thorough examination of the learning resources.

High expectations are also communicated to students through the feedback given by the instructor. It has been our experience that students appreciate the frequent, specific feedback on their performance provided in PBL projects. The personalized feedback in combination with the integrative essays students complete after each project generally stimulate students to begin to define personal learning objectives in addition to those designated in the project specifications. This often results in their applying themselves with at least equal effort and more focused attention in subsequent projects. Students report that, over time, they begin to work smarter as well as harder.

Confidence in the PBL methodology and attitudes of experimentation, patience, supportiveness, and high expectations form an underlying affective foundation for implementing PBL in the classroom. These attitudinal dimensions provide signals of the instructor's beliefs and intentions to students. While the instructor needs to create a learning environment that invites and supports student risk-taking, the environment must reflect high expectations and standards for student success. As noted, the teacher accomplishes this through attention to students' transition to PBL as well as through other features of the PBL methodology. In the absence of such a learning environment, PBL does not fully attain its potential for student engagement and learning.

In the following sections of this chapter, we discuss the instructional decision-making and behaviors of the instructor as he or she implements PBL in the classroom. We organize the discussion in terms of salient considerations and actions of the instructor before, during, and after using a PBL project in class.

The Instructor's Role Before a PBL Project

As we discussed in the chapter on project development, PBL involves a significant front-loading of time and attention on the part of the instructor. Front-loading includes not only the development of new PBL projects, but also the preparation of materials and other resources prior to instructional sessions. Here we review decisions for the instructor to consider prior to an actual PBL instructional unit. These decisions must be made in the course of (1) selecting the PBL materials, (2) reviewing and preparing PBL project materials and logistics, and (3) preparing the class for the PBL project.

Selecting the PBL Materials

Selecting the materials represents a critical task in implementing PBL. The PBL materials act as a substitute for the instructor's input during the course sessions. They not only convey the content of the course, but also provide a structure for the students' learning activities. Thus, professors must select PBL materials with care.

Whether the instructor intends to use PBL projects developed elsewhere or self-authored projects, he or she must first consider the content for the course or professional-development program. The instructor, therefore, reviews a range of projects in light of his or her curricular goals. When reviewing projects for course selection, the instructor will find it useful to pay attention to six features: (1) learning objectives, (2) prerequisite skills and knowledge, (3) relevance of the problem to the intended audience, (4) role of the primary actor in the project, (5) problem context, and (6) time constraints.

Learning Objectives

First among the instructor's considerations is whether the learning objectives are appropriate to the course goals. A review of the stated learning objectives in the PBL project specifications can clarify this issue quickly. Assessing the fit between course goals and learning objectives tends not to be quite as straightforward as it sounds, however, since PBL projects are interdisciplinary in nature. If the instructor is still teaching within a traditional curricular format (that is, courses organized in terms of academic disciplines), the instructor may need to adopt a more flexible attitude toward the goals of the course.

Therefore, we recommend that instructors look beyond the learning objectives during this phase of project review. At times, the stated *learning objectives* for a project may not fit exactly into a conventional course. However, the *problems* and associated content knowledge presented in the project may be highly salient to students in the particular program. In this instance the instructor might choose to adapt the project by reframing the learning objectives, by reshaping the learning resources, or by reframing the course goals.

Prerequisite Skills and Knowledge

It is also useful to consider whether students lack any of the prerequisite skills that are explicitly indicated by the project author or are implicit in the project specifications. If so, the teacher must identify ways to support the students in completing the project. This issue is particularly applicable in professional-development settings where a PBL project may be used in a stand-alone fashion.

For example, we have developed a high level of respect for the utility of the Interaction Method (Doyle and Straus 1982) as a tool to assist our students in managing their group work. When we have used a PBL project outside the context of a course curriculum, we have found it worthwhile to provide a one-page overview of meeting-management roles. Even when groups choose not to fully implement the model, it provides some support to facilitate the group process (see the project *Because Wisdom Cannot Be Told,* Appendix A).

Similarly, a PBL project may require students to write a memo, role play a supervisory conference, or make an oral presentation. If they haven't already learned these "action skills," we add supplementary learning objectives and learning resources to the project.

Relevance of the Problem to the Intended Audience

Since the problem is such an essential part of PBL, students must perceive the situations represented in the selected projects as highly salient. The nature of the problem, the role of the primary actor, and the context in which the problem is presented shape the students' perceptions of the project's salience. For example, the salience of the project *In English Please* may vary depending upon the degree of ethnic and linguistic diversity in the communities where administrators work.

Knowledge of what constitutes salient problems for students may at times require prospective evaluation of students' needs by the instructor. Organizing the curriculum in terms of the problems rather than disciplinary content may at times lead instructors to change their view of what ought to be included in a course. When this occurs, it should be viewed as a positive development. Such curricular adaptation indicates that the instructor is viewing the disciplines as being placed in service to the profession, rather than the opposite.

Role of the Primary Actor in the Project

Who is the primary actor in the project? Most of the PBL projects we have developed to date place participants in the role of a school principal. To the extent that the nature of the course or program varies, the instructor may vary projects to incorporate a range of managerial roles.

In Stanford University's New Pathways to the Principalship program, the students occupy a variety of educator roles. They do, however, share a common goal of aspiring to school-level leadership positions. In this case, all PBL projects focus on the principalship.

At Vanderbilt, PBL projects have been used with K-12 administrators, teachers, university administrators, human-service administrators, and corporate human-resource developers. At times, these classes have been organized homogeneously (for example, all K-12 school administrators). At other times, a single course has included students who either aspired to or held a range of different managerial roles. In these instances, to the extent possible, projects have been selected that reflect the career goals and problems of the various administrative positions.

In considering this issue in project selection, our experience with mixed groups has been that it is of primary importance that the students view the problems presented in the project as salient. If the problems presented are highly salient and the forms of managerial resolution of the problem are comparable, students do not tend to be overly distracted by the role of the actor in the context. Of course, there may also be limits in terms of applicability of the project when the managerial position differs too dramatically from the current or future position of the students.

Problem Context

The context in which the problem is presented is also salient to the audience. If the nature of the problem presented in a project is too narrow, part of the audience may feel shut out and disengage. Consideration of the problem context attends to several issues, all of which involve reviewing projects based on the needs and interests of the students.

First, the instructor must consider who will attend the program. Even in programs that serve a single role group, such as principals, the project problems should not be overly narrow. For example, a project that focuses specifically on implementation of the middle-school concept may be viewed as less relevant by administrators at other levels. Of course, a training institute for middle-school principals might find such a project quite pertinent. PBL projects can be adapted by reframing the problem and adjusting the products and resources. A project on middle schools could be reframed as a problem of organizational restructuring and change implementation. This might increase the salience for participants from a wider range of school levels.

We must emphasize that when the problems presented are sufficiently broad in impact and common in occurrence, school administrators at a variety of levels generally feel equally engaged by the project. That is, high-school administrators do not appear to be overly distracted by projects that involve an elementary-school context.

At times the instructor may need to select projects for courses that include students who aspire to or hold leadership positions in various types of school and nonschool organizations. As we noted in the previous section on the primary role of the actor in the project, in these instances, we vary the context of the PBL projects in the course to include as many organizational types as possible.

Time Constraints

Finally, the instructor must consider time constraints relevant to curriculum implementation. These constraints commonly take two forms. First, there is a recommended duration for each project. The teacher must coordinate the time allotted for the selected projects into a course or institute schedule. Particularly at the beginning, we have found it good policy to err on the side of giving too much, rather than too little, time to a project.

The second type of time constraint concerns the format of the course or training program. We have implemented PBL in university courses meeting in several time formats: weekend classes, classes meeting twice a week for three-hour sessions, and classes meeting twice a week for one-hour-and-fifteen-minute sessions. We have also used PBL in one- and two-week professional-development institutes (see Hallinger and Greenblatt 1990).

Our experience suggests that it is possible to adapt PBL to a wide variety of time formats. However, certain time formats are more effective than others. We find that students work most productively when a project is scheduled for substantial blocks of time (for example, two to three hours per session) over a period of one to three weeks. Shorter time blocks limit or complicate efforts to conduct the extended simulations that are part of certain projects. Longer sessions over a very short period (such as a weekend) offer time for extended activities but limit students' capacities to coherently integrate concepts from readings into their understanding of the problem. Few of these constraints are insurmountable. Successful implementation does, however, require the instructor to plan for the specific constraints that are associated with the different time formats.

Reviewing and Preparing PBL Project Materials and Logistics

After selecting the PBL project materials to be used, the next step involves reviewing the resources and mechanics of the project. Here the instructor must consider how to conduct the project within the constraints of the particular setting.

We have already discussed one issue relevant to implementation—time constraints. However, each PBL project has multiple components that require similar attention. The tasks commonly involved in preparation for the classroom include (1) selecting readings and other resources (old and new ones), (2) arranging for the provision of human resources, (3) preparing materials, (4) preparing the physical environment, and (5) obtaining equipment.

Planning for these well in advance of the class session is critical to the smooth functioning of a PBL project and also to student success.

Review the PBL Project

As instructors, we find it imperative to read all the resource materials before assigning a project. This enables us to understand the content of the project as conceived by the author. Since it is likely that the project will relate to an area of the instructor's expertise, this process often leads to the selection of additional readings and/or replacement of indicated readings. If time constraints are particularly severe, the instructor can reduce the reading load by identifying certain readings as optional and others as required.

Arrange for Human Resources

We typically engage two types of human resources in PBL projects. First, we solicit the assistance of practitioners for role plays associated with the products of various projects. For example, one project, *Present Your Case!* (Bridges with Hallinger 1992, pp. 134-43), has the participants making a presentation to school-board members concerning selection of an AIDS-education program. In this and other projects, we identify willing occupants of the role in question to take on the relevant role in the project performance. We send them a copy of the project specifications ahead of time, along with instructions concerning our expectations for their part in the role play. We have found that practitioners are eager to assist in this fashion, but that engaging their effective participation requires clear communication of our expectations and attention to scheduling well ahead of time.

A second way in which we engage a range of human resources in PBL is through the appointment of expert consultants. These may be professors or practitioners who have particular expertise with respect to the issues presented in the project. We often recruit one or more expert consultants for a project. We send them a copy of the project specifications and include brief guidelines on how to conduct themselves in response to student questions. Students are given the consultants' names, contact information, and their areas of expertise.

When using consultants, students must initiate the contact and prepare specific questions ahead of their appointment. We generally ask that students limit their consultations to thirty minutes. This saves our consultants' time and forces students to sharpen their thinking and focus their questions beforehand.

We have experimented with a variation on the use of consultants through videotape. We have developed videotapes for two projects in which expert consultants share their thinking about the problems in the project. Again, we recruit willing experts and send them a copy of the project specifications. Then, during a videotaped session, we ask them to think aloud from their perspective as a researcher or practitioner. They discuss which problems seem most salient to them and how their point of view would shape their approach to solving the problem. For the project *Something Old, Something New, and the Principal's Blues,* we produced a videotape that incorporates expert thinking from several different disciplines (organizational culture, adult development, change implementation, school effectiveness, staff development, problem-solving) that bear on the project problems.

These videotapes can be provided to students either during the unit as an instructional resource or at the conclusion of a project to supplement the instructor's debriefing. When providing students with the videotape as a learning resource, the instructor should, however, caution them to follow the same guidelines as with other resources. They should explore the nature of the problems as a group before examining the videotape.

Prepare Project Materials

Once the instructor is familiar with the project's specifications and mechanics, he or she must prepare the actual learning materials for students. Between the readings, project specifications, and various other handouts, the paper management involved in PBL can become complex. We have found through trial and error that looseleaf binders work well for storing PBL materials since they allow for the easy insertion of photocopied readings and the additional resources that students accumulate during a project.

Since projects draw from an interdisciplinary set of resources, it is simply not feasible to work from a text. This complicates matters since the instructor is forced to draw on materials that require copyright permission. We allot extra time for this process when working with campus or commercial copy centers.*

Prepare the Physical Environment

We cannot overstate the importance of designing a physical learning environment conducive for PBL. The instructor must attend to both room assignment and classroom preparation. The classroom environment must facilitate the conduct of group meetings and problem-solving sessions. A room with tables and chairs that can be rearranged for small-group work is optimal. Depending upon the size of the class, the instructor may also want to provide breakout rooms for meetings, since classrooms are often noisy with three or more groups meeting simultaneously (though we have done this with some regularity). We schedule classroom space up to one year in advance to ensure that the room size and furniture are appropriate for PBL.

Plan for Use of Necessary Equipment

The equipment needs for PBL projects vary. In most instances, however, butcher paper or pads with easels, marking pens, masking tape, and a videotape player are needed. Some projects may also require a camcorder for videotaping or a computer lab.

Assign Students to Teams

The final preparation prior to actual implementation of a PBL project is the assignment of students to PBL groups (also referred to as project teams). The instructor forms teams that work independently for the duration of a single PBL project. As we noted in chapter 1, the unit of instruction in our version of problem-based learning is the *project*. Like project task forces in the workplace, the project teams come together for a single PBL project and then disband. New project teams are formed for subsequent projects.

---

*For the convenience of both instructors and students, the ERIC Clearinghouse on Educational Management includes reading materials with the projects it has published. The Clearinghouse obtained reproduction releases from the copyright holders and paid the necessary fees, which are included in the price instructors and students pay for the projects. As a result, portions of commercially published books and complete journal articles, often totalling in excess of 100 pages, are contained in both instructor and student editions.

The instructor assigns students to their groups. We actively resist student entreaties to let them form their own groups or to continue in the same groups over several projects. We believe this sets up unhealthy dynamics within the class for students who aren't actively sought out by others or who may have been unhappy with their groups. We tell our classes that as an administrator you must learn to work with a variety of types of individuals and you do not always have the option of picking who will participate with you on a project team.

While this has been our practice, not all PBL instructors follow this same guideline. Some find that keeping groups together for several projects, or for a semester, allows groups to learn different lessons about group functioning. For example, during the course of several projects students may observe the growth of group norms concerning participation. Or, members may be able to observe the resolution of certain dynamics among individuals within a group.

There is not one right answer to this question. These are, however, some of the salient issues. The individual instructor should consider these issues and then decide which method of assignment to follow. Students can learn important lessons concerning group functioning from either approach.

Although we have worked with groups as small as four and as large as ten, we try to keep the group size to between five and seven persons. Our experience suggests that this range allows for optimum levels of student participation in the project. This is partly influenced by the type of group process we seek to create.

We encourage our students to use the Interaction Method (Doyle and Straus 1982) as a means of organizing and managing their team meetings. This technique places three group members in specialized roles: leader, recorder, facilitator. Therefore, at least five people are necessary to have a group that can fully utilize the method.

Larger teams allow full utilization of the Interaction Method. However, we find that students' opportunities for individual participation in the team's learning activities begin to fall appreciably when the group size exceeds seven. This is an important consideration in PBL, since the goals differ from those of a project task force in the workplace. A task force is primarily concerned with production of a project. In PBL we intend for the project team to produce a product and to optimize individuals' learning during the process. Unless properly managed, we find that large teams provide a less conducive learning environment for our students.

Over the course of a term, we keep track of who has assumed the roles specified in the Interaction Method, particularly that of group leader. We try to ensure that as many students as possible have an opportunity to assume the leadership role for a PBL project. At the outset of a project, we hand out a list of group assignments and specify who among the team members will assume each of the three roles (that is, leader, facilitator, recorder). The team leader remains leader for the duration of the project. If the team chooses to use the Interaction Method, the other two roles rotate among the group members periodically over the duration of a project (for example, after each group meeting).

The composition of the groups is, in and of itself, a potentially useful vehicle for student learning in the area of group dynamics. As our students have commented, the very process of problem-based learning affords future leaders with an opportunity to learn from the dynamics that arise naturally as students tackle a problem. As one of our students observed, "An analysis of group processes is necessary for a real understanding of leadership and group dynamics. I learned the most from my groups' discussions of how we worked together" (Hall 1994, p. 7).

The instructor may choose to place particular stress on this aspect of the students' learning. At times we have used the *Personal Style Inventory* (Keirsey 1984; see sample syllabus in Appendix C) as a means of identifying students' personality types. Subsequently, we ask students to identify their personality-type designators within their groups and to attend to these over the duration of a course or program. This can lead to useful learning concerning how different types of people interact in groups.

Several professors who participated in training institutes we have conducted in PBL have suggested other conceptual frameworks that could be used for similar purposes. With or without such a framework, the dynamics of team participation represent an important opportunity for student growth in both cognitive and affective domains. Therefore, to optimize student learning, we urge instructors to give attention to issues of group formation prior to classroom implementation.

Summary

The successful implementation of PBL requires considerably more advance attention to materials review, selection, and preparation as well as logistical planning and support than most teachers are accustomed to providing. The teacher's attention to the aforementioned aspects of instructional design contributes to the creation of a learning environment that supports students' ability to succeed in PBL. Our version of PBL draws explicitly on the power of cooperative group learning. But cooperative learning requires a well-designed learning environment. One of our undergraduate students noted this in an essay after several PBL projects.

> Peabody is known on the Vanderbilt campus as the *home* of group work in classes. But sometimes the professors just put you into groups and it's neither clear why we're doing groupwork nor how we're supposed to learn in a group. In this class we have been given a method for working and learning as a team. This has increased our productivity enormously. I am even beginning to use some of these techniques when we have to work in groups in other classes.

Inadequate attention to development of the learning environment decreases both the efficiency and effectiveness of student learning in PBL. This reinforces the importance of paying explicit attention to the process of the groups' teamwork and learning.

We find that institutions vary widely in their ability to provide the logistical support and flexibility that are absolutely necessary for the successful classroom implementation of PBL. Particularly at the initial stages of classroom implementation, the instructor must expect to budget considerably more time for planning before the course begins. This includes time not only for materials preparation, but also for learning how to arrange for the necessary resources (for example, classroom space, photocopying of text resources, camcorder).

Advance preparation, however, is a key piece of the answer to the question posed by the staff developer at the outset of the chapter. It is through careful attention to these aspects of front-loading that the instructor is able to achieve a seamless unfolding of a PBL project. In the next section, we discuss the type of instructional decision-making that characterizes the teacher's role during the actual classroom sessions that comprise a PBL project.

The Instructor's Role During a PBL Project

In considering the role of the instructor during a PBL project, we assume that the instructor has already introduced students to problem-based learning, projects have been selected, materials have been prepared, team membership has been determined by the instructor, and the class is ready to proceed. Thus, the focus of this discussion is on the instructor's decision-making during the process of a typical PBL project.

Introducing the PBL Project

The logistical arrangements for a given course or program shape how a project is actually introduced to students. At the outset of a project, the instructor must inform students of their assignments to project teams and of their roles (if any). Then we generally provide a brief overview (about fifteen minutes) of the project before releasing the teams to begin their work. The overview explains the importance of the project's problem to the work of administrators, the desired learning objectives, the nature of the products the students will develop, and the time constraints under which the class will complete the project. We then distribute project materials (that is, the specifications, readings, videotapes, and consultant contact information) and signal teams to begin their first project meeting.

We keep in mind several things that bear on the logistics of introducing a PBL project. First, we make our introduction brief, simply providing an overview and clarification of expectations. This is not—despite a natural desire—the instructor's golden opportunity to make up for lost time on stage. The goal is to give students the essential information and then let them get started on their own.

Second, whenever possible, we do *not* distribute readings in advance of the project specifications. As we have emphasized throughout this volume, in problem-based learning the problem comes first. The problem acts as a stimulus for the subsequent learning of concepts and skills. Instructors need to resist the temptation to have students get a head start on the readings. The instructor should maintain control over the resources until groups have formed and teams have had time to review the project specifications. Review of the readings and other resources should come *after* students have examined the problem, individually and hopefully in their groups.

A third suggestion is to structure the introduction of a PBL project to facilitate project planning. We have found that teams function more effectively when the team leader has developed a preliminary plan for the project *before the first team meeting*. Students often do not see the importance of project planning at first. In one integrative essay, an undergraduate student noted that when in the role of group leader she "felt strangled by the very idea of developing a project plan." However, after several experiences of participating in project teams that had project plans of varying degrees of coherence, she concluded that although planning was not something she enjoyed, it was necessary for group effectiveness.

If the instructor wants team leaders to develop project plans, three steps will facilitate this. First, the instructor should explicitly state the expectation that team leaders will formulate and turn in a copy of their project plan. In the absence of a clearly stated expectation, we find that most students will not take the time to plan the project systematically.

Second, the instructor should provide a time structure that facilitates planning at the outset of the project. This may be accomplished in a variety of ways. For example, the instructor can distribute the product specifications to the group leaders with the request that they develop a preliminary project plan for the group's first meeting (that is, when the rest of the class receives the materials). Or the instructor can schedule the introduction of a new PBL project for the last hour of a class session so that the teams have a chance to form, to read over the project specifications, to exchange contact information as desired, and to assign responsibilities for the next meeting (for example, readings, review of videotapes). The team leaders then work toward developing and distributing project plans for discussion in the subsequent class session.

Third, the instructor can provide a planning form for use by students (see Appendix D). They can this use form or develop their own model.

Developing Classroom Norms That Support Problem-Based Learning

Earlier we noted that to facilitate effective learning in PBL, the instructor must allow students to make mistakes. It is equally important that the teacher create a learning environment in which students develop habits that foster learning from their mistakes. Much of the instructor's effort in creating the PBL environment is bent toward providing students with the tools they need to function as productive learners in the absence of teacher-directed instruction. The front-loading of time and attention to project development, materials preparation, and logistical support is designed to provide a framework for learning in which students can succeed. In addition to these structural components, several classroom norms also support PBL.

Using Time Effectively

When students work in a PBL environment, they become acutely aware of time—how much (or little) is available, alternatives for using it productively, how it is running out. Once they become responsible for their learning, they begin to approach time as a scarce and valuable resource. The instructor can foster development of a positive norm by emphasizing that students are responsible for deciding how they will use their time within the duration of the project (that is, until the date and time when products are due).

As noted earlier, the instructor also cues students to the importance of treating other peoples' time as valuable by issuing guidelines on the use of consultants in the project. Finally, we introduce students to a framework for thinking about the management of one's time (Covey 1989) through a PBL project, *Time Management: The Work of the Principal* (Bridges 1994).

Developing a Problem-Focused Orientation to Learning

In PBL it is also the instructor's task to assist students in becoming *problem-focused* in their learning. We ask students to examine all learning resources in light of the problems presented in the PBL project. This strong focus contrasts sharply with the more typical book-report mentality with which students *cover* their readings.

A problem-focused exploitation of readings, videotapes, and consultations raises the issue of *application* in students' minds during the course of their learning. Students become more sensitive to the important impact of context on the application of knowledge. In theory, this should enable them to retain and subsequently apply this knowledge in the workplace.

As an example of this, it is often the case that students *jigsaw* readings as a means of dividing up the labor for a PBL project. When this cooperative-learning technique is used, we remind students that their note-taking and reports should highlight how the reading illuminates issues raised in the problem. Typically, the instructor must verbally cue students to this focus on the problem several times before they begin to develop it as a positive habit.

Personalizing Learning

Another norm we encourage is for students to personalize their learning by identifying personal learning objectives in relation to PBL projects. This, again, is a habit that the instructor must stimulate and then reinforce; it tends not to develop naturally for most students. The instructor can ask students to define their learning objectives at the beginning of a project. However, in practice, we have found that students' awareness of their learning needs more often emerges over time.

It is, therefore, important for the instructor to reframe issues that may arise in the integrative essays of students as possible personal learning objectives. In PBL, students have multiple opportunities to engage in administrative thinking and behavior. Thus, students may identify an issue as salient in one project and then formulate this as a personal learning objective in subsequent projects.

Resourceful Learning

Another norm that enhances effective learning in a PBL classroom is student resourcefulness. The emphasis on self-directed learning requires students to become more active seekers of information. Although this feature is admittedly less prominent in the problem-stimulated version of PBL, it is still possible to encourage student resourcefulness as learners.

In conventional classes, students often treat knowledge as if it is bounded by the resources provided by the instructor. This places students in a very passive role in relation to the subject matter. Teachers reinforce this perspective by admonishing students against sharing information with each other or seeking information from people outside the classroom who might have the answers. A curriculum is often said to have been *covered* when the students have been exposed to the readings selected and approved by the instructor.

In PBL, we prompt students to seek out useful information wherever it may be found. This begins in their learning teams. One of the characteristics of high-performing teams is their capacity for exploiting the knowledge and skills of team members. We, therefore, encourage students to make the identification of the team's resources, as they relate to the problem, a routine step in the problem-solving process they use.

We also invite students to use people in the workplace who may have expertise concerning the issues that arise in a PBL project. Thus, this norm and the norm of approaching knowledge in a problem-focused manner are both geared toward teaching students to use knowledge as a tool for problem-solving. We believe that if students become resourceful learners in the classroom, they will be better prepared to become resourceful leaders on the job.

Self-Monitoring

Finally, students need to develop the ability to monitor themselves individually and collectively. The integrative essays are designed to assist in individual reflection. We use peer feedback as a vehicle for the groups to monitor their process. During each team meeting, students provide each other with specific, concrete, nonjudgmental feedback. We ask our students to save five minutes at the end of each meeting for a debriefing. At this time team members identify what went well during the meeting, how they performed in their roles, and what they can do to improve team performance in future meetings.

These learning norms are mutually reinforcing. Together they foster students' capacity for working successfully in a cooperative-group-learning environment. As Hall (1994) observed in her study of a PBL class, these norms begin to exert a powerful influence on students' engagement in their learning.

> This self-monitoring element became a habit for them and they saw the value of it in other areas of their lives as well. The various facets of the monitoring process further instilled the recognition that the [teacher's] desired goal was for them to learn how to learn, not just make a grade or only recall specific outcomes from a project for a test. . . . This inspired and required continual reflection by the students individually and also stimulated communication among the group members.

Interacting with Students During the Project

In a PBL classroom, the teacher lives in the background for over 90 percent of the project's duration. This represents one of the hardest transitions for instructors. PBL places instructors in a position whereby they convey their expertise through selection of materials and learning resources, through limited interventions during class, and through their feedback to students. This suggests the need for teachers to develop both a reservoir of self-discipline and a repertoire of new instructional skills that foster students' learning. Although the instructor lives both physically and metaphorically in the background of a PBL class, the instructor still fulfills a number of tasks during a PBL project.

Provide Content Information

The instructor acts as a resource to groups as they grapple with the problem and the content of the resources. It is, however, interesting to note that although we make ourselves available to students during a project, students are often reluctant to draw on our knowledge in relation to the project. Therefore, we explicitly remind them that they may seek our input on the problem. When doing so, however, they must follow the same guidelines as we specify for their use of consultants. They must prepare specific questions. As consultants, our job is to clarify issues, not provide answers as to what they should or should not do.

This is a particularly sensitive type of interaction in that students have a finely honed instinct in hunting for *right answers*.

Given years of classroom experience, they assume that there is a right answer hidden in the instructor's mind. Thus, when the instructor responds in these interactions, it is useful to use a Socratic style: asking questions, directing students to other resources, and raising alternative points of view, rather than offering prescriptions.

Act as a Process Observer

The instructor also acts as a process observer of the project teams. Typically, we rotate among groups, spending some time with each to get a sense of how they are proceeding. Occasionally a group may be bogged down due to problems in the process of the group's work. At these times, an intervention may be appropriate.

Before intervening with a group, we force ourselves to stop and ask, "Is the content of my intervention *critical* either to the group's learning how to deal with this process problem (or their understanding of the problem)? If so, is it likely that they will overcome the current obstacle without my intervention?" As instructors, we have found it necessary to cultivate personal strategies such as this to maintain the self-discipline needed to stay within our own role during class sessions. Now we are more likely to take notes concerning the problems students encounter and share our thoughts with them either verbally or in writing *after* the project has been completed.

Clarify Project-Specific Issues

During the project, the instructor may also need to clarify student roles or project-specific issues. When using the meeting-management techniques, it is often necessary, particularly early in the students' experience of PBL, to clarify the responsibilities of the different roles in practice. At times, the instructor may also need to clarify a particular component of the project, for example, the nature of the product expectations or assumptions concerning the problematic situation.

Consult with Students on Individual Issues

Students may request time to meet with the instructor individually during the course of a project. We encourage this as much as possible. In some situations, for example, with an undergraduate class, we have even found it useful to require group leaders to schedule meetings with the instructor during the project to review progress and issues that have arisen.

Monitor Time

During the project the instructor must monitor and communicate with the teams concerning the time flow. The teacher must assess whether and how to modify the time allocated for the project. This matter of time tends to require the most attention the first time that an instructor uses a project. However, some projects have specific role-playing activities that have been scheduled with outside resource persons. In such cases, the instructor must monitor the progress of groups to maintain the overall schedule for the project.

Debrief the Class

The last task is the debriefing that occurs at the conclusion of the project. As with other features of PBL implementation, time constraints may shape when the final debriefing is held. If the project concludes with a *public* performance, such as a presentation to a school board or a supervisory conference held with a teacher, the instructor may debrief with the class immediately after the performance. If the product is a written plan or memo that the instructor must first review, this may not be possible. In these cases, we hold the debriefing during the subsequent class session.

There is a tension here between the instructor's desire to take some time to review and reflect on the students' products and a need to provide fresh feedback to students. PBL generates a great deal of individual and group investment in final products. Instructors should capitalize on this by providing feedback as soon as possible following conclusion of the project. This helps students obtain closure and motivates them for the next project. It also allows them to incorporate the instructor's feedback into their reflections for the integrative essay.

The group debriefing should refer students back to the learning objectives and recast the completed project in terms of the administrative role that is being performed. In the debriefing, students will want a reaction from the instructor concerning their performance. Again, we have found it important to avoid the right-answer syndrome.

As we discuss in the chapter on student assessment, the instructor should emphasize the positive aspects of the students' performance and raise possible consequences of the proposed actions. The instructor may focus students' attention on content issues that still need clarification as well as aspects of the problem and points of view toward the solution that may not have been considered. Project debriefings should also solicit questions and unresolved issues from students.

Summary

During the course of a PBL project, the instructor must learn to live comfortably in the background. To counter the fairly predictable feelings of anxiety concerning the apparent lack of a role, we recommend two strategies. First, we suggest that the instructor remember the amount of work that went into the creation of the PBL environment in which the students are working. Although this strategy is not action-oriented, it may relieve some of the unproductive self-doubt that can emerge during class on the part of the instructor.

The instructor can also use the observations of groups as an opportunity to gather data on the team performance. We incorporate these data into the formative feedback that we provide to students following completion of the project (see Appendix E). Students frequently express the viewpoint that the instructor's new role is at least as informative as the old one when they receive concrete, useful feedback on their work during a PBL project. This, in turn, builds the instructor's confidence in the legitimacy of a way of teaching that changes the public role of the teacher so dramatically.

The Instructor's Role After the Project

Two important aspects of the instructor's role occur following the project: providing written feedback to students and reviewing their feedback to the instructor. All of our PBL projects incorporate integrative essays in addition to the project-specific products. The integrative essays serve to stimulate metacognitive processing of the students' experience and refocus their learning from the project. Somewhat surprisingly, students come to value writing the integrative essays, despite their frequency. As Hall found, "They enjoyed having to think about the process of their work and saw [the essays] leading to individual growth and recognition of group progress" (1994, p. 7). The depth of students' reflection in these essays is often startling to the instructor (see, for example, the essay "Student Response to the PBL Classroom Environment" included earlier in this chapter). The essays stimulate such considerations quite naturally.

Feedback to the Students

In response to these serious efforts by the students, we approach our feedback as part of an extended *conversation* with students that unfolds over the course of the term or institute. Normally we return the essays to students with comments as well as questions for their further consideration. The feedback on the essay also represents an opportunity for the instructor to reframe issues raised by the student as possible learning objectives for subsequent projects.

The project-specific products are also reviewed by the instructor and returned to students with comments. We generally provide written feedback to each group on their group product (such as a group's presentation or plan) and to individuals for individual products (such as individually written memos). However, when a PBL project calls for an individual product—for example, a written memo to the supervisor—we may also write a memo to the whole class discussing issues that arose in the class's products as a whole.

Consistent with our previous comments, we maintain a positive and constructive approach to providing students with feedback on the project's products. The "Feedback to Students" on the project *Write Right!* in Appendix E illustrates the tone and nature of feedback that we strive to provide. We discuss these issues at greater length in the chapter on student assessment.

Student Feedback to the Instructor

The explicit solicitation and incorporation of feedback from students is part of the process of continuous improvement that we seek to model for students. We solicit feedback from the class regarding the project verbally in the debriefing as well as through the "Talk Back" sheets and integrative essays. We already noted the function that the two-page essays serve for students. In addition, these essays provide the instructor with insight into the students' personal experience of the project. This feedback is invaluable in understanding how to adjust the project's use in the future.

The "Talk Back" sheets provide a second source of directed feedback for the instructor concerning the project. We ask students to answer these questions anonymously. These sheets solicit data concerning both the extent to which students feel the project achieved its objectives and ways in which to improve it. We often type the students' comments from the "Talk Back" sheets in summary form and distribute them to the class so they can see how others responded. We sometimes discuss these comments with the class. In addition to the practical value of these data for the purpose of project revision, the act of soliciting and sharing the information indicates to students that the instructor values their input.

After reviewing the content of the integrative essays and the "Talk Back" sheets, the instructor begins to consider modifications to the project. We find it useful to record these notes for future use as soon as possible after the project so they don't become blurred by the next project's activities.

Conclusion

In this chapter we have tried to convey the nature of the instructor's role in problem-based learning and to offer specific suggestions for teaching in a PBL classroom. A problem-based-learning environment is radically different from traditional teacher-directed, simulation-based, and case-based classroom environments. Following her study of a PBL classroom, Hall concluded, "What surprised me was the degree to which each person in the class described the atmosphere of the class as being remarkably different from any other class they had ever experienced" (1994, p. 15).

The creation of this type of learning environment is an instructional goal in PBL. As we have sought to convey, however, it takes considerable front-loading of effort and attention to the selection of subject matter, planning of logistical details, and the development and support of group-learning norms. Reaching the goal of self-directed learning on the part of students does not occur unless student roles and expectations have been clearly established. While the instructor does not appear to be a central figure in the PBL classroom, PBL is unlikely to attain its potential unless the instructor creates a structure and a climate that support self-directed learning.

Student Assessment

I n the spring of 1993 we offered a week-long institute on problem-based learning for twenty-four professors drawn from all regions of the United States and one country in Southeast Asia—Thailand. Prior to the institute, we provided participants with a list of possible topics and activities and asked them to indicate their level of interest in these topics. Somewhat to our surprise, participants uniformly expressed an interest in learning about student assessment.

As we prepared our discussion of this issue, we thought it might be useful to contrast student assessment in a problem-based-learning environment with what transpires in conventional educational administration programs. Once again we were surprised. We discovered that scholars in our field rarely discuss student assessment. When they do, the discussions reveal little, if anything, about how professors evaluate students. Rather, these abbreviated discussions criticize the lack of rigor and issue a call for higher standards (for example, Murphy 1993; Griffiths, Forsythe, and Stout 1988).

We then turned our attention to the literature on medical education to learn how future physicians have been evaluated in a problem-based-learning environment. As we anticipated, the literature on student assessment in this field was somewhat richer and more informative (for example, Boud and Feletti 1991, pp. 243-

90). This literature sensitized us to a range of assessment issues. However, it provided few, if any, definitive answers, because student assessment in medical education remains a controversial, hotly debated issue. The current state of evaluation in this field has been succinctly characterized by Swanson, Case, and van der Vleuten (1991): "Despite recognition of the importance of assessment among problem-based-learning advocates, there is little agreement on methodologies for assessment."

Our discoveries unsettled us. We realized that we had no definitive answers to this important issue. Moreover, we could not draw on the literature in medical education to support our views about student evaluation, and we had no sense of how our participants evaluated their own students. Based on our knowledge of teacher evaluation, we anticipated that the participants would hold strong views about student assessment and that their views would differ from one another.

How should we approach discussing this topic in light of these discomforting circumstances? We decided to address issues of philosophy, rather than technique. Our approach, as we anticipated, sparked a lively discussion. We pushed a "hot button" that forced participants to confront what one participant late in the discussion characterized as "their comfort zone." Some participants obviously were uncomfortable with evaluation that did not provide the instructor with ironclad assurances that students knew the content. Others were uncomfortable with evaluation that failed to place a premium on analysis. Still others were uncomfortable with evaluations that did not result in a "grade." Many were uneasy about providing detailed feedback to students about their performance.

We suspect that our discussion of student assessment in this chapter will similarly test the reader's "comfort zone." Unlike our discussion in the institute, we have chosen to treat issues of technique, as well as philosophy. As in previous chapters, we sprinkle our discussion with numerous examples. The reader should bear in mind that our thoughts about student evaluation are written in sand, not chiseled in stone. We continue to experiment with different approaches and to question how we have chosen to approach this important issue. We invite readers to join our quest for a sensible resolution to this problem and to stretch "your comfort zone."

Philosophical Orientation

Our philosophy of student assessment has been shaped in part by the intensity of the problem-based-learning environment and the performance anxiety that this intensity creates. These features of our version of PBL were highlighted for us by Dr. Michele Marincovich, director of the Stanford University Center for Teaching and Learning. At the end of the first summer of the Stanford Prospective Principals' Program, we invited Dr. Marincovich to meet with students and to solicit their views of the program and how it might be improved. Following this meeting, she wrote:

> The first [feature that stands out] is the palpably high intensity of the program. All participants, with one possible exception, feel it in a very stressful way.... Closely allied to this concern is the obvious preoccupation among members of the group with their success as students. Although they are all established professionals already, it is clear that they are suffering great performance anxiety. (Bridges with Hallinger 1992, pp. 130-31)

Since we want evaluation to serve learning and now recognize that the intensity of the PBL environment is quite high, we have striven to create conditions within the classroom that seek to ease, rather than aggravate, this intensity. We reason that we can enhance performance and learning by creating a learning environment in which it is safe to make mistakes and to fail. Toward this end, we emphasize to students that mistakes and failure represent valuable learning opportunities. Moreover, we stress how our own experience with PBL has shown us that more learning occurs when things work out poorly than when they go well. Paradoxically, current failure breeds later success.

Besides striving to create an environment that regards mistakes as learning opportunities, we also attempt to foster a supportive learning environment. Toward this end, we front-load our feedback to students with considerable praise for aspects of their performance that warrant approval or commendation. We have discovered that when one looks for positive aspects of a performance, one can find them no matter how marginal the overall performance is. One indicator of our success in creating a supportive learning environment is hearing students say (as they have said), "They make us feel good even when we screw up."

In our effort to produce an optimal level of anxiety and to promote transfer of learning, we think it is important to assess students on the basis of performance tests. Although these performance tests are contrived, they are sufficiently realistic that students do not experience them as contrived.

If students are to benefit from these performance tests, we believe that it is essential for them to receive feedback that aims to improve their future performance. Operating from this perspective, we emphasize formative, rather than summative, evaluation. We are convinced that a grade conveys little useful information and may divert students from seriously considering how to improve their performance. The grade, not the performance, becomes the students' overriding concern. To rivet the students' attention on performance, we endeavor to highlight it, rather than the grade (replaced by pass/no credit). When we and others provide feedback, everyone attempts to identify where the performance is particularly strong and where it may need improvement.

Although we prefer a pass/fail approach to grading students in PBL courses, we recognize that this approach may not suit other professors, or it may be prohibited or discouraged by some institutions. To conform with institutional requirements, Hallinger has graded students in the undergraduate courses in which he used PBL. However, he uses pass/fail at the graduate level since the institution allows professors to use this approach with graduate students.

His experience with the traditional grading system in his undergraduate PBL courses yields several observations and suggestions that may be of interest to those who use grades in a PBL environment. First, his experience reinforces the notion that grading raises the level of student concern. In combination with the intensity of PBL, this heightened concern can interfere with student learning. Second, it seems that the instructor can reduce this problem by providing timely, focused formative feedback to students. To the extent that students receive adequate formative feedback and see that the instructor takes this aspect of evaluation seriously, they seem to adapt their expectations as well.

Third, when using grades, it becomes particularly important to review and adjust, as needed, the nature of assessment exercises. For example, this may mean including some additional knowledge-review exercises (discussed later in this chapter). It may also mean changing the mix of assessment exercises to include individual and group assessment exercises in every project. For example, some of the projects we have developed include only "group" products (excepting the integrative essay, also discussed later in this chapter). When using PBL under a traditional grading system, the instructor's task in grading will be eased by ensuring that there are individual as well as group assessment activities incorporated into projects throughout the course.

Upon completion of their formal preparation, students for the most part will not receive frequent, detailed feedback about the quality of their performance. Instead, they will rely heavily on their own informal assessments as a means for ensuring their continued growth and improvement as administrators. To assist students in developing their skills in making these informal assessments, we deem it important to cultivate habits of self-evaluation and reflection.

Finally, since we embrace the notion that evaluation should serve learning, we regularly involve students in assessing the quality of the learning experiences that we provide. When students participate in evaluating their program, they can provide instructors with the information needed to determine how the learning experiences may be improved and made more worthwhile and meaningful for students. Evaluation that aims to improve learning should include assessment of the program, as well as the students.

Test Design

In line with our formulation of PBL, we design performance tests that mirror the realities of the workplace insofar as possible. Since the basic unit of instruction is a project and students use class time to meet in the project teams, each class session constitutes a performance test. As students work on a project, the activity affords an opportunity to observe how they perform in various roles (leader, facilitator, recorder, and team member), set agendas, deal with conflict, solve problems, organize and plan, and communicate. In short, the process of instruction that we use represents an ongoing series of performance tests. These tests permit students and faculty alike to gauge each student's progress in learning the administrative skills emphasized by the program.

In addition, we design each project to culminate in a product or a performance that resembles what students will actually be doing in their future roles. Thus far, we have included a wide array of products and performances in the curriculum. By way of illustration, we have designed the following kinds of performance tests:

- Making a formal presentation to a Board of Education about how a controversial topic (AIDS education) should be incorporated into the local high school's curriculum

- Designing and implementing a set of procedures for choosing among three finalists for a teaching position

- Planning and implementing an IEP (Individualized Educational Plan) conference with the types of people who ordinarily attend such conferences

- Observing a classroom teacher and preparing a written record of the teacher's performance for the teacher's personnel file

- Reviewing the personnel file of a teacher who has a record of poor performance and preparing a remediation plan and a notice of unsatisfactory performance

- Developing a school-improvement plan and defending it before a superintendent, director of staff development, and business manager

- Identifying what the major task is for a newly appointed School Bilingual Advisory Committee and developing an agenda for the first meeting

Each of these performance tests is highly contextualized. Students are provided with detailed information about the particular situation in which the focal problem for the project occurs. (See Bridges with Hallinger 1992, pp. 134-59, for examples.)

Types of Evaluation

In considering how the students' performance on these tests should be evaluated, we have found it useful to think of evaluation in terms of who *structures* the assessment and who *judges* the performance. Student evaluation can be structured by either the instructor or the student; similarly, the quality of the performance may be judged by either the instructor or the student. The persons who structure the evaluation make decisions about what aspects of a performance should be evaluated and what means should be used to evaluate these various aspects. Individuals who judge the performance make decisions about the strengths and weaknesses of the performance and how it may be improved. By conceptualizing evaluation in this way, we arrive at four types of evaluation, as depicted in figure 1.

Thus far, we have relied substantially more on type 1 evaluations (instructor-structured and instructor-judged) and type 3 evaluations (instructor-structured and student-judged) than type 2 (student-structured and instructor-judged) and type 4 (student-structured and student-judged) evaluations. Since the first two types of evaluation have figured prominently in most projects, we later discuss the various forms that these types of evaluation have taken and provide numerous examples of what we have used to assess student performance. Consistent with our sparing use of type 2 and type 4 evaluations, we devote less attention to these two types.

FIGURE 1

Four Types of Student Evaluation

		Structured by...	
		Instructor	*Student*
	Instructor	Type 1	Type 2
Judged by...			
	Student	Type 3	Type 4

Focus of the Evaluation

To date, we have targeted evaluation to the goals identified in chapter 1, namely:

1. Familiarity with problems inherent in future professional role

2. Possession of knowledge relevant to these problems

3. Competence in applying this knowledge

4. Proficiency in problem-solving

5. Skill in implementing solutions to these problems

6. Capacity to lead and facilitate collaboration

7. Ability to manage emotional aspects of leadership

8. Proficiency in self-directed learning

Our attention to these various goals has been uneven, however. For the most part, we have taken the goal of "familiarity with problems" for granted. In the near future, we plan to assess whether the problems that we have incorporated into our PBL projects are the ones that figure prominently in the work of our graduates. We may discover that there are other problems that warrant greater attention than some we have been using. We also have devoted little attention to assessing the students' proficiency in self-directed learning. In our later discussion of instructor-structured and instructor-judged evaluation we describe an approach that has been used in medical education and seems suitable in our context as well.

Student assessment has not been perfectly aligned with these eight goals. Given the experiential nature of problem-based learning, students often obtain insights into their own previously unrecognized attitudes, beliefs, predispositions, and shortcomings. These insights can become occasions for profound personal and professional growth. We sensitize students to this possibility and encourage them to use their experiences in PBL as a way to achieve greater understanding of themselves.

Forms of Student Assessment

When discussing the various ways in which students have been (or will be) assessed, we have organized the discussion around the four types of evaluation that we described earlier. Since we have already discussed how students evaluate each PBL project by means of "Talk Back" sheets (see Appendix A), we will not repeat our discussion of that form of instructor-structured and student-judged evaluation.

Instructor-Structured and Student-Judged Evaluation

During the past five years we have experimented with several different forms of this type of evaluation: integrative essays, protocols, models or examples, knowledge-review exercises, and probing questions. In the near future we plan to use prospective, as well as retrospective, forms of this type of evaluation.

Integrative Essays

As we noted in the chapter "Developing PBL Instructional Materials," students prepare an integrative essay following each project. We provide varying amounts of structure to students regarding the issues to be addressed in these essays. In some cases, we ask students to discuss what they have learned during the project and how they might use the knowledge and skills in the future. In other cases, we provide students with an extended list of questions (see chapter 2, pp. 45-46) and invite them to choose one or more of these questions to discuss.

To provide the reader with a clearer sense of the content of these essays, we reproduce below two essays written by students following their participation in the project *Children with Special Needs*. During this project, students plan and conduct an IEP (Individualized Educational Plan) meeting with a parent, a special-education teacher, a resource specialist, and a math teacher. The person from the project team who conducts the meeting is chosen at random a few moments before it takes place. By randomly selecting the person shortly before the meeting, we create a measure of individual accountability. Since everyone has an equal chance of being selected, each person comes prepared to conduct the meeting. In addition, students are required to select a handicap that they live with for an entire day. The instructors also adopt a handicap for a day to model the importance of this experience.

Although these two students approach their essays somewhat differently, one obtains a sense of what both learned, how their attitudes changed, and what experiences were instrumental in producing the learning and changed attitudes.

INTEGRATIVE ESSAY NUMBER 1: CHILDREN WITH SPECIAL NEEDS

Of all the areas of education, I was most oblivious to the rules and regulations of special education. This was despite having a special day class next to mine at my school and having a series of Learning Disabled kids in my class. I acted like most of the teachers at our school; I commiserated about "those" kids and worried about their placements, but I didn't even know what a special day class was. I guess I was in denial in the sense that I didn't really want to know. As a result, I looked at this project with some trepidation because I didn't want my ignorance to show. Fortunately however, this project presented me with the steepest learning curve thus far. The three principal areas in which I increased my knowledge were gaining an understanding of the legal requirements of special education, how to conduct an IEP, and how, as principal, I can help meet the needs of learning disabled kids.

I only vaguely held the idea that by court decision the primary goal of educating students with special needs was to place them in the most appropriate, least restrictive environment. After reading through the arguments for such placement, it now seems obvious; after all, most people desire acceptance by their peers, etc..., why not a student with special needs? The differences between special day classes and resource classes were finally made clear. (If the student is mainstreamed in at least 50% of his/her classes then by law they should be transferred from special day class to resource class.) I learned that one of the guiding principles of Public Law 94-142 is to have the parent involved in making educational decisions concerning the student. Again, this is obvious to me now, but up until the day before the conference we were going to do a "tell and sell," because we didn't know any better! The due process vs. complaint procedures were also a revelation to me. Previously, I considered them to be one and the same. The list of new knowledge I discovered is long and useful. The most useful "legal" knowledge that I take from this experience is that when a student is mainstreamed, that student is the responsibility of the classroom teacher and no one else. It hurts a little when I think back on the LD students I've accepted into my class, yet considered them less than full partners in the class. Unfortunately, I was sure those students belonged to the special education teachers, and so inadvertently I probably lessened their learning experience. It will not happen again.

The IEP conference role playing demonstrated to me how important it is to include the parent(s) in the educational decision making process. This hit me particularly hard as my son has had difficulty learning to read and we worry he is dyslexic. His teacher tells us it's too early to tell and she thinks he's just a late maturing kid, but I agonize nonetheless. Lupe (a fellow student) once told me that whenever he has a conference with a student he always considers what he would do if that student were his own child. Those are words I intend to live by, especially in handling an IEP. We may be the educational experts, but that mother was the expert considering her child. Due to the very sobering effect this experience had on me, I can't imagine taking an IEP lightly in the future.

When I read in the specifications for this project that I needed to simulate a handicapping condition, I was really put off. I got angry and complained about what inconvenience this simulation would cause. Each day I got up and planned to have hearing difficulties, and each day I found a reason why I couldn't perform my simulation that day. Being a little thick, awareness that inconvenience is the point didn't strike me for about 10 days. When I finally followed through and put the cotton in my ears, it proved to be not as bad as I had imagined. It was, well... inconvenient. It just added to an already high level of stress. The saving grace was that I knew seven o'clock would come and I could get on with my life. At the risk of sounding melodramatic, for many others seven o'clock never comes. It just makes you feel lucky.

Overall this project proved to be the most rewarding for me on many levels. It has been particularly helpful in building a special education knowledge base and in modeling the IEP meeting process. Most importantly, I think the project modified my view of students with special needs, and I will take a much improved attitude back to my school in the fall.

INTEGRATIVE ESSAY NUMBER 2:
CHILDREN WITH SPECIAL NEEDS

During this project, I learned valuable information regarding the legal and educational aspects of special education. I learned how to plan and conduct an IEP conference, and gained a deeper understanding of how a handicapping condition affects an individual's life.

On the Legal and Educational Aspects of Special Education

Although laws like P.L. 94-142 clarified many of my questions regarding special education for the handicapped, I found their content a challenge to read. The laws were particularly unclear on the issue of parental consent. One of the four questions I missed on the knowledge-review exercise concerned this issue. As the law reads, parental permission is required whenever a child is to be individually evaluated and whenever a child is first placed in a special education program. What about altering a child's special education program? Apparently, parental permission is not required. Does this mean that had we not tested John Jones (the student), we could have moved him without his mother's permission?

In the future, I will certainly refer to the literature on the educational aspects of special education. I found it to be of great value. The article describing the principal's role in mainstreaming contained essential information. The authors of this piece make important recommendations about securing appropriate accommodations for handicapped children, changing negative attitudes pertaining to special education, and supporting and integrating all staff on this issue.

I was particularly moved by the writers' comments regarding the importance of setting a good example as a principal. It has been my experience that even though school leaders (and teachers) may claim to support special education programs, their actions say otherwise. The authors make this point in their article. They describe how some principals they observed in their study, spoke loudly and slowly to all handicapped students as if they were all hard of hearing. The authors recommend that to overcome that ill-at-ease behavior, principals should have more interaction with their handicapped students. I agree. It's difficult to appreciate the differences among people until you have made an honest and genuine attempt to understand them. The authors feel that it is important to see heterogeneity among students as a method of teaching about life. There is a line in this article which in my opinion summarizes the main point of this project. In describing the actions of a principal who supports mainstreaming at her school, the authors write: "To her, mainstreaming was synonymous with good education."

On Planning and Conducting an IEP Conference

After completing this project, I feel that extensive preparation for an IEP conference is crucial. This preparation should not be limited to the time immediately preceding a conference. A principal must be prepared for crises (like having to facilitate an IEP conference at the last minute) by being informed. Being prepared means keeping information on how mainstreamed students are progressing. Gathering this information may encompass getting to know one's special students by listening to them, observing their interactions with other students, and knowing about their lives outside of school. This last recommendation may also include having information about students' parents and their general views about the education of their children.

Conducting an IEP conference a la PPP (Prospective Principals' Program) differed from what I have seen. My experiences in this area have been limited to short meetings where the psychologist and other special education staff explain test results to parents and tell them where their child will be placed. It has been very direct. I have felt uneasy about this approach because there is no attempt to inform parents about their rights in this process. The IEP staff that I have worked with seem to have resigned themselves to the idea that it is not worth the trouble to inform parents.

The collaborative approach that our group planned to take for this conference was a challenge to carry out. There were times when I felt we weren't collaborative at all and tried to force Mrs. Jones (the parent) into accepting our recommendation. I think that at this point interruptions began and voices were slightly raised. It is important then to be aware of our actions. In theory we supported collaboration, but in practice we came across as much more direct. This contradiction is related to the kind of mixed messages that the authors of the article on the role of the principal had warned against. This experience leads me to the realization that learning does not end once it's been rationalized in the mind. *Applying ideas and putting them into action brings further awareness.* [Italics added for emphasis.]

On Being Handicapped for a Day

My day as a physically challenged individual further supports the idea that actual experience produces deeper learning. [Italics added for emphasis.] For my handicap, I taped my fingers on my right hand together. Beside the frustration that came with my inability to carry out tasks such as typing on the computer, the most troubling aspect of this experience was that I felt stigmatized. I felt very uncomfortable being stared at when I could not do such things as complete a check to pay for my groceries at Safeway. As uncomfortable were the stares the Jack in the Box attendant gave me when I handed her money with my taped hand. Their stares seemed to say to me that I was obviously flawed. I began to feel flawed. It really drove home the point that people's actions toward the handicap often speak louder than words. These actions are devastating to the self-esteem of the handicapped person.

Conclusion

This project has made a lasting impression on me. Not only has it raised my awareness about the procedural aspects of special education, but it also led me to examine my own beliefs and biases about handicapped individuals.

Protocols

Studies in the field of medical education have demonstrated the value of protocols in promoting behavioral change among physicians. Protocols consist of instructions, guidelines, or checklists that professionals may use to guide or monitor their performance. Given their proven effectiveness in effecting behavioral change, we have developed a limited number of protocols that our students have found useful in evaluating their own performance.

For example, early in the curriculum we introduce students to a set of standards that can be used to judge their memos. (See the accompanying sidebar "Feedback: Written Communication.") We have incorporated these standards into a protocol that students are expected to use when drafting and evaluating the memos they prepare in the various PBL projects included in the curriculum. The standards embedded in the protocol are described in the reading material that we supply students.

FEEDBACK: WRITTEN COMMUNICATION

Note: The numbers in parentheses refer to pages in Munter, *Guide to Managerial Communication*. If a check precedes an item, you need to work on that aspect of your writing.

Message strategy (pp.19-21)

_____ direct approach (front loading; see Sweetnam)
_____ indirect approach

Organization and design (pp. 42-49)

_____ white space
_____ headings and subheadings
_____ parallel forms
_____ typography

Coherence (pp. 52-57)

_____ preview for introduction
_____ previews for lengthy sections
_____ conclusion
_____ transitions
_____ document design

Paragraphs (pp. 56-57)

_____ Start with generalization; subsequent sentences support generalization

Models or Examples

Since projects culminate in a product or performance, we sometimes provide students with examples of completed products at the end of a project. We ask students to study this model, contrast it with their own product, and then comment on the strengths and weaknesses of their products.

By way of illustration, in the project *Dealing with Problem Teachers* we ask students to prepare a remediation plan and a notice of unsatisfactory performance based on a tenured teacher's personnel file. This file contains several classroom observations, reports of conferences between the principal and the teacher, two annual evaluations, and summaries of the assistance provided to the teacher in the past. When students have completed their remediation plan and their notice of unsatisfactory performance, we provide them with a plan and a notice provided by an experienced administrator. Students read the example and comment on their own products in light of this example. Excerpts from the example that we supply students are reproduced below.

—SCHOOL DISTRICT
Any City, USA

TO: Mr. Teacher
FROM: Ms. Principal

SUBJECT: Notice of Unsatisfactory Teaching Performance

As we discussed in our recent conference, your teaching performance since coming to ___ School has been seriously deficient in the areas of student progress, instructional techniques, and management of learning environment. Although we have discussed specific problems and strategies for remedying them, you have been unable to correct these deficiencies over the three semesters we have worked together. Your overall performance remains unsatisfactory.

The intent of this memo is to support your efforts to correct these deficiencies by again outlining the areas of unsatisfactory performance, giving specific examples of the problems and means to correct them, and proposing an assistance plan. I am committed to working with you to solve these problems, but I must inform you that if they are not corrected by June 1, 1994, I will take action to have you dismissed from your teaching job in this District.

AREAS OF UNSATISFACTORY PERFORMANCE

Student Progress

You do not clearly communicate academic expectations to students and parents. Parents report that the purpose of assignments and the way you use them to judge student progress are not clear. You assign to students tasks that are below their level in quality or quantity, leading to a general lack of student involvement or attentiveness. For example, I have observed the following:

- On 5/27/93 a small group of students were given the task of completing a ditto and copying a poem. All finished early and were given no other task to work on....

Instructional Techniques and Strategies

....

Management of Learning Environment

Your classroom is physically disorganized. Bookshelves, tables, and the children's work area are frequently cluttered. There is no clear arrangement of student desks. You have not established clear routines for collection of homework or getting materials ready for learning, and your expectations for conduct during seatwork or completion of unfinished work are not clear to students. For example, I have observed the following:

....

REMEDIATION PLAN

Improvements Required

In order for your performance to be judged satisfactory, you must demonstrate the ability to:

- monitor student progress and communicate it effectively to parents and students

- plan and deliver instruction that is engaging and challenging to students and that makes effective use of class time

- maintain a physical environment and behavioral expectations that enhance learning opportunities for students.

....

Resources for Assistance

To assist you in meeting these requirements, the following resources are available to you:

- At your request, Mrs. Mentor (or other District mentor of your choice) will provide the following assistance:

    — review and comment upon your lesson plans, prior to submitting them to me

    — observe your class and offer feedback and/or suggestions

- I will release you from your class for 45 minutes at a time each Tuesday during this six-month review period for the purpose of observing your grade-level partners and other staff members. We will plan these observations together, and Mrs. Mentor or I will accompany you on some of them.

....

You have 10 working days to make any signed written comments you wish to have attached to this document. After that time, it will be placed in your permanent personnel file.

Knowledge-Review Exercises

Some of the projects that we have included in our curriculum contain technical information. To ensure that students understand this material and can apply it in their future professional roles, we have prepared knowledge-review exercises that we distribute at the beginning of the project. Students may elect to use these exercises as pretests or posttests or both. At the end of the project we distribute an answer key. Students use this key to review their understanding of the material. An example from the *Children with Special Needs* project appears below.

EXAMPLE OF KNOWLEDGE-REVIEW EXERCISE

Test item: Rank order (from 1 to 5) the following special education placements in terms of the type of educational environment provided for handicapped children. Designate the least restrictive environment as "1" and the most restrictive as "5."

— placement in a special day school serving only handicapped children

— placement in a resource room for 60 minutes per day

— placement in a self-contained special education classroom within a regular elementary school

— placement in a speech therapy program with 30 minutes of group articulation therapy twice weekly

— placement in a homebound tutoring program

Test item: Jose is an eight year old who recently moved to the school from the rural area of Northern Mexico. He speaks little English and does not know how to read in English or Spanish. He tells his bilingual teacher that only last year did he begin to attend school on a regular basis. His teacher notices that he continually reverses his numbers and seems unable to pay attention for more than five minutes at a time. He is unable to carry out a three-step command even when the directions are given in Spanish. Jose's teacher suspects that he might have a specific learning disability. The school psychologist does the appropriate testing and concludes that Jose does not have a learning disability. Based on what has been described in this paragraph, why do you think the psychologist came to that conclusion?

Test item: You are the principal of an elementary school. Mary, a second grader, has been referred to your office three times this week for refusing to do her work in class. While she is in your office, you ask her to copy her spelling words from the book. She complies, but her work is messy and filled with inaccuracies in spelling and the formation of the letters. She labored 10 minutes in copying five words. You then ask her to read a short passage from the second grade basal reader. Her oral reading is halting and she continually says "saw" for "was." She is unable to answer correctly any questions about the passage she has just read. Mary has always struck you as someone who gets along well with her peers and teachers, but you've noticed that since the beginning of second grade she looks increasingly confused as she sits in class. You suspect that she might have a learning disability. You schedule a conference with her teacher. What are three questions that you might ask about Mary's academic abilities?

Probing Questions

At the conclusion of some projects, we provide students with a set of key questions to consider in relation to their final products or performances. These questions stimulate students to think about concepts that they may have failed to use in dealing with the focal problem and to consider important constraints or resources that they may have overlooked.

For example, students in the *Something Old, Something New, and the Principal's Blues* project develop a three-year school-improvement plan to address a range of challenges confronting an elementary school with a changing population, declining test scores, and aging staff. When students complete this project, we provide them with several questions to ponder about their school-improvement plan:

1. What activities did the team design to meet the needs of teachers at different career/adult developmental stages?

2. How was change introduced—through formal structures, informal processes, or both? Why? What might be the consequences of introducing change through other means?

3. How were the change activities sequenced over the three years, and how does the sequence support the notion of developmental change?

4. How does the plan address the superintendent's primary concern: raising student achievement scores?

5. What strategy was used to obtain support from the district administrators, both in the content of the plan and in the meeting?

Students then discuss how their plan addressed or failed to address the issues that we raised.

Student Preferences

As we accumulate a body of PBL projects, we can provide students with some choices about the projects they will study. To facilitate their making informed decisions, the instructor can prepare an annotated list of projects and ask students to rank order their preferences. In this way, students can judge prospectively how projects meet their needs and interests and maximize their opportunities to learn in a PBL curriculum. By supplying students with an annotated list of PBL projects, the instructor also assists students in developing their self-directed learning skills.

Instructor-Structured and Instructor-Judged Evaluation

In most projects we use type 1 (instructor-structured and instructor-judged), as well as type 3 (instructor-structured and student-judged) evaluations. Our type 1 evaluations usually center on the process events that occur during each meeting of the project team and the products or performances that cap each project. For the most part, these evaluations are guided by the goals described earlier in the section "Focus of the Evaluation." One of the goals requiring more attention in future evaluations is the students' skills in self-directed learning.

Process Activities

In line with the major goals of the program, we attach considerable emphasis to evaluating students' performance during team meetings. These evaluations tend to focus on one or more of the following topics: the skills of team participants in carrying out their various roles (leader, facilitator, recorder, or group member); the skills of the team in framing and solving problems; and the ability of team members to use the knowledge appropriately in dealing with the focal problem. To illustrate the forms that these evaluations take, we discuss several examples from our own classroom experiences with PBL.

In one of the initial PBL projects in our curriculum—*Meeting Management*—we introduce students to the Interaction Method (Doyle and Straus 1976) for conducting meetings. Students read about this method and are expected to use it in all subsequent projects. During the numerous meetings of each project team, we evaluate the students' skills in performing the various meeting roles (leader, facilitator, and so forth). For example, we look at various indicators of their skills in performing the facilitator's role, such as:

- clarifying the process for dealing with each topic on the agenda

- managing the meeting time efficiently

- maintaining a neutral stance during the meeting

- promoting the participation of all team members

- resolving conflict

- focusing the group on the purpose of the meeting

- protecting group members from attack

During the meetings of the project team, we also gather data on the distribution of participation within the meeting as an indicator of team functioning. We use these data to answer questions like the following: Are there any gender or ethnic differences in the frequency of participation? Is anyone dominating the discussion? Are there any silent, noncontributing members? Are contributions of group members being valued differentially on a regular basis? How is the team dealing with disagreement?

When monitoring the team's problem-solving process, we use a number of indicators of its effectiveness. Is there evidence within the problematic situation to support the team's definition of the problem? Has the team incorporated a solution into the statement of the problem? To what extent has the team identified the constraints and the resources that are relevant to dealing with the problem? Whose interests (narrow vs. broad) are being addressed by the way in which the problem has been defined and resolved? Has the team anticipated potentially negative consequences for the various alternatives and estimated the seriousness of these consequences? How reasonable are the definition of the problem and the proposed course of action in light of the facts included in the description of the problematic situation? Has the team made any unwarranted assumptions (for example, about the underlying causes of the problem)?

We generally organize our feedback to students around two main themes. First, we identify those aspects of their performance that are especially praiseworthy. Our list of positives generally is a long one. Second, we raise a small number of "things to think about." Since we do not wish to overload students with facets of their performance requiring improvement, we intentionally limit our feedback to two or three major items. This approach is feasible since we have the opportunity to provide feedback on a regular basis over an extended time.

Culminating Products and Performances

As we have noted, each project culminates in a major product or performance. When providing critical feedback, we strive to frame it as follows:

- Here's what we see...

- Here's why it concerns us...

- Do you see it that way or some other way?

- If the student agrees with our assessment, we explore how the performance might be improved. If the student disagrees with our assessment, we probe why the student feels that way. Our subsequent actions depend on the views expressed by the student and whether we consider them valid.

By way of example, during one of the projects and the culminating performance, we noticed that the leader displayed two radically different patterns of behavior. When things were going well, the leader exhibited a functional pattern of behavior—listened attentively, reacted positively to challenges from others, elicited suggestions about how to improve the product, and was considerate and gracious. However, when things were not going well, the leader displayed a dysfunctional pattern of behavior—became defensive, interrupted others, argued for his own point of view, and adopted a testy manner.

Following the project, we met with the leader and described the two patterns of behavior we had observed. We further explained why the discrepant behavior patterns concerned us by pointing out how various patterns of behavior breed similar responses. If the leader adopts a dysfunctional pattern, the followers are likely to manifest a similar pattern. This potentially destructive cycle of leader behavior and follower response undermines a group's ability to reach high-quality, acceptable decisions. We then provided the student with a copy of the videotape that showed how he was behaving under different conditions and invited him to view the tape with the purpose of determining whether he agreed with our perceptions. He later met with us and expressed full agreement with our feedback. We, in turn, explored various ways in which he might deal with the problem that we had identified and he had owned.

In our experience, when students "own" a problem or short-coming, they can make significant progress in overcoming it, just as the student in this situation did. However, if students blame the problem on someone else or circumstances beyond their control, their performance rarely improves. By inviting students to discuss whether they view the situation the way we do, we facilitate their owning the problem. In the process we sometimes discover that we have misperceived the situation. Our openness to this possibility further contributes to students' owning the problem on those occasions where we have perceived the situation accurately.

Self-Directed Learning Skills

In the near future, we plan to use a version of the "triple jump exercise" (Painvin and others 1979) to assess the students' self-directed learning skills. As part of this exercise, the instructor presents students with a problem. The student reads the problem and meets with the instructor to discuss the potential learning issues inherent in it. Following this discussion, the student identifies and reviews the relevant resource material. When students complete this phase, they meet again with the instructor to discuss the conclusions they have reached about the problem, the resources they have consulted, and the knowledge they have acquired that has proved useful in understanding and dealing with the problem. This "triple jump exercise" affords an opportunity to assess the students' problem-solving skills and knowledge of the problem area, as well as their self-directed learning skills (Swanson, Case, and van der Vleuten 1991).

Student-Structured and Student-Judged Evaluation

We also have experimented a few times with this type of evaluation. Generally, these evaluations have taken but one form. In several projects we have required students to construct a protocol for judging their own performance and to include in this protocol indicators that should be used when judging their own performance. In some instances, students have also asked their peers to provide feedback using this protocol. The reactions of students to these opportunities are typified by this student's comments:

> The video taping session was a valuable experience. I am embarrassed to admit that I have not taped myself making a presentation or teaching before. The fact that it was the first time for me made it intimidating. The creation of our own feedback sheet made it a more valuable experience as it forced us to concentrate on specific areas for evaluation and improvement.

Student-Structured and Instructor-Judged Evaluation

On a few occasions students have submitted work and invited us to comment on their performance. These students signal particular aspects of their performance on which they desire feedback. Their performances take a variety of forms (for example, videotaped conferences or presentations, memos, written plans).

Conclusion

In this chapter we have discussed one of the major challenges facing those who elect to use problem-based learning, namely, student assessment. Our discussion has centered on the philosophy behind our approach and the formal types of assessment that we have used. We have slighted the informal assessments that naturally occur in a PBL environment. Once students become familiar with one another and the philosophy that we have adopted, these assessments frequently take place. In our experience, students can be quite candid with one another, and this informal feedback promotes self-awareness and behavioral change.

As our understanding of the various facets of PBL increases, we tend to direct our attention to issues that are not fully resolved in our own minds. Student assessment is clearly one such issue. As the number of PBL users increases, we fully expect that some of them will push the frontiers of student assessment beyond where we are currently. Perhaps, our discussion will assist this growing body of users to create more effective and efficient methods for promoting student learning through evaluation.

Using Problem-Based Learning as a Focus for Ed.D. Research

In this book, we have sought to convey how problem-based learning can become a vehicle for building meaningful connections among research, theory, and practice in the classroom. In this chapter, we turn our attention to a different programmatic feature in the preparation of educational leaders, the Ed.D. dissertation. We both teach at institutions that offer the Ed.D. as a degree option for professionals seeking advanced study in educational administration. The Ed.D. dissertation was originally conceived as the *capstone* of the professional doctoral program in educational administration. We both have worked with students for whom the dissertation experience achieved this status. Unfortunately, more often than we care to admit, the Ed.D. dissertation fails to provide a demonstration of the student's ability to apply knowledge in a professionally productive and academically sound manner.

When this is the case, the result is unsatisfactory for all concerned. Many of our Ed.D. students, respected professionals with significant responsibilities by day, tell us that they often feel frustrated by their doctoral experience. Their craft knowledge and professional expertise find too few outlets for expression, especially at the dissertation stage, when they undertake independent doctoral research.

As professors, we have experienced a similar and persisting frustration. When confronted with the challenge of mentoring Ed.D.

students, we have chanted the "professor's litany" many times, both solo and in unison with colleagues:

- Why haven't they learned how to identify a researchable problem?

- Why can't our students read the literature critically?

- How did they get through their coursework without ever learning how to employ inquiry and research tools in a real project?

- Why can't they produce a product that will see the light of day upon completion?

Although it may come as a surprise to some, this is the case even in our doctoral programs. Despite the fact that our institutions draw high-achieving professionals into our Ed.D. programs, their success at the dissertation stage is sometimes disappointing. In these cases, the process leads to an unhealthy expenditure of effort when viewed in light of the outcomes.

Our interest in exploring the use of PBL projects as the focus for doctoral dissertations arose from a desire to develop more productive linkages among research, theory, and practice in the context of our professional students' doctoral research. The idea of drawing on PBL as a tool for dissertation study was an unanticipated outcome of our own immersion in PBL as a classroom-based instructional strategy. During the process of developing PBL materials for our classes, it gradually dawned on us that we were engaged in a powerful form of practice-oriented inquiry. *We found that the process of developing PBL projects demanded that we draw on the very same capacities for critical synthesis, systematic inquiry, and application of domain-relevant knowledge that we professed as the goal for our professional doctoral students.* We were impressed with the positive results of this inquiry process for ourselves as professors. Consequently, we became increasingly intrigued with the idea of exploring the potential of PBL for extending the learning of our professional doctoral students at the dissertation stage.

In this chapter, we share the results of our experimentation. We begin by delineating our assumptions about the professional doctorate in educational administration, particularly as it concerns the Ed.D. dissertation. Next, we outline the research and development methodology that we have used as the framework for incorporating PBL into the Ed.D. dissertation. Then we present several specific options for incorporating problem-based learning into the design of professional doctoral research projects. We draw examples from the experience of using PBL as the focus for research with several students in Vanderbilt University's professional doctoral program. The chapter concludes with a discussion of the benefits and implications of mentoring Ed.D. projects such as we describe in this chapter.

Professional Doctoral Research

Graduate programs in educational administration face a persisting challenge to successfully meet the expectations of two different organizational cultures: the professional workplace of schools and the academic environment of the university. The negative consequences arising from the failure to meet this challenge are legion and have been discussed at length by scholars in the field (Bridges 1977; Griffiths, Stout, and Forsyth 1988; Hallinger and Murphy 1991; Murphy 1993). We do not intend to explore in further detail the nature of this problem. Instead, we seek to offer an alternative that meets at least some of the needs identified for such programs with respect to classroom instruction.

Here we extend our conversation by exploring how PBL can be integrated in Ed.D. research. Consensus on distinctions between the Ed.D. and Ph.D. is hard to come by in our field. We start with the assumption that these doctoral degrees are, however, characterized by different academic and career goals for students. We briefly discuss the implications of these differences as they play out in our professional doctoral programs.

Assumptions Concerning the Ph.D. Dissertation

The Ph.D. draws its intellectual orientation from the academy and seeks to prepare its recipients for careers as researchers. Commonly, the criteria for the Ph.D. dissertation spell out the need for students to contribute to the "creation of new knowledge." Generally, this involves the development of a conceptual or theoretical framework that is applied toward the analysis of a salient problem drawn from theory, empirical research, policy, or practice.

Graduate coursework for the Ph.D. reflects these expectations. Typically, we expect Ph.D. students to develop a broad range of theoretical knowledge within a discipline of their choice, to achieve competence in a particular research methodology, and to explore in depth a domain within the field of educational administration. A goal, not always achieved, is for the student's research to generate findings of sufficient methodological validity and academic interest to result in publishable reports.

When viewed from this perspective, the Ph.D. dissertation represents a meaningful *transition ritual* within the university culture. Through the process of conducting their research, students learn the nature of academic work and the norms that govern academic careers. The Ph.D. product—the dissertation—demonstrates the student's ability to conduct independent research at acceptable standards. Both the process and the product prepare the student for entrance into the professoriate.

Assumptions Concerning the Ed.D. Dissertation

In contrast with its elder sibling, the Ed.D. degree was created to meet quite educationally different goals. Where it is offered, the Ed.D. is intended to provide opportunities for practitioners to develop the capacity to apply knowledge from theory and research to problems of policy or practice. The creation of new knowledge is not generally a stated goal of Ed.D. research, though this distinction is often fuzzy in practice.

The career goal of Ed.D. recipients in educational administration generally remains within the sphere of practice. For many, the Ed.D. represents a stepping stone to a higher position as an educational administrator. Consequently, professional doctoral students tend to view dissertation research as an academic requirement for completing the doctorate, rather than as an experience that will have instrumental value in their future work.

The program of study in the Ed.D. reflects the mixed pedigree of the degree. Ed.D. programs provide courses concerned with the practice of educational administration as well as courses that reflect adaptations of social-science theory and research methods associated with the various academic disciplines. Unfortunately, the academic compromises inherent in these programs are such that students seldom obtain the indepth training needed to conduct independent research at a reasonable level of quality. Nor do they generally receive training that graduates of such programs perceive as being relevant to their roles as practitioners. In a sense, the nature of our compromise limits our ability to capitalize on the strengths of either domain.

The outcomes of Ed.D. research are similarly confused. The expectation that Ed.D. dissertations will result in publishable reports is not generally realistic. Students simply do not receive adequate preparation in research methods to carry out high-quality, social scientific independent research. When viewed as a group, Ed.D. studies tend to be narrowly focused, atheoretical, and highly limited in terms of methodological sophistication. Consequently, such studies make few recognizable contributions to the empirical research literature, theory, or practice (Bridges 1982).

Therefore, we conclude that the Ed.D. dissertation is often a transition ritual devoid of meaning for professional students. The Ed.D. dissertation reflects neither the work tasks nor the professional norms that characterize the career paths of professional students (Bridges 1977). Thus, these dissertations do not serve an instrumental role by contributing to knowledge of the *practice* of school administration. Nor do they fulfill a socialization function by preparing students for the normative expectations that characterize the higher administrative roles they may enter after obtaining the doctoral degree.

The compromises inherent in the conduct of Ed.D. dissertations often result in dissatisfaction for both students and professors. Many of our students contend that the dissertation experience fails to meet their needs as practitioners. As professors, we often feel an acute intellectual discomfort with the quality of Ed.D. dissertations. This result is almost inevitable given the confused goals and design of the degree program.

For the purposes of this chapter, we will assume that the Ed.D. dissertation is a vehicle for achieving a purpose that reflects the goals of the professional doctoral student. Graduates of Ed.D. programs in educational administration should be able to demonstrate their ability to apply appropriately research, theory, and craft knowledge to problems arising from educational policy and/ or practice. The Ed.D. dissertation represents an experience through which students can demonstrate their achievement of this goal.

In the following sections of this chapter, we explore how problem-based learning may be used as a vehicle for assisting professional doctoral students in educational administration to accomplish this goal. As we have emphasized in our discussion of problem-based learning as an instructional strategy, we view PBL as one option among those available for dissertation study. Moreover, the options that we present here do not represent the full range of potential directions that might be taken with PBL in the context of doctoral research. They are simply the ones with which we have experimented to date.

Research and Development Methodology

As noted at the outset of this chapter, we more or less stumbled upon the idea of using PBL in the context of doctoral research as a result of our own project-development efforts. Reflection upon our own experience in project development led us to conclude that the same process could have applicability for our professional doctoral students. This led to a search for a research model that would allow us to incorporate PBL into doctoral research.

The model that we chose to work with is referred to as research and development (R & D). Borg and Gall describe educational research and development as "a process used to develop and validate educational products" (1989, p. 782). Their description of the R & D model immediately suggests its relevance to the PBL process and its appropriateness for our purposes.

> One way to bridge the gap between research and practice in education is to do R & D. It takes the findings generated by basic and applied research and uses them to build tested products that are ready for operational use in schools. . . . R & D increases the potential impact of basic and applied research upon school practice by translating them into usable educational practices. (Borg and Gall 1989, p. 782)

It is in the nature of this model that the research and development process results in products that can be used in the field. At times, the R & D process may also generate original contributions to knowledge, but that is largely a byproduct, not a primary goal, of this research model. In their presentation of this methodology, Borg and Gall offer an extended example and conclude:

> [In this case] the developer was able to make a contribution not only to practice but also to research knowledge. . . . The results of the field test contributed new knowledge, and raised new questions [of theoretical and empirical interest]. . . . In planning an R & D project, you too may find yourself considering alternatives about such matters as product design, product content, and target audience. It may be possible to compare several alternatives through informal or systematic experiments incorporated in the field test phases of the R & D cycle. (1989, p. 801)

When we reviewed these characteristics of the R & D model, the design seemed particularly well suited to our stated goal for the Ed.D. dissertation. Moreover, the R & D cycle seemed to mirror the inquiry process we had been using to develop PBL projects. Our subsequent experimentation with the R & D process supports both of these initial suppositions.

The Research and Development Cycle

Borg and Gall have identified ten steps in the research and development process (see table 3). These steps reflect a systematic plan of inquiry designed for product development and testing. As we began to explore the educational research and development process more closely, it became apparent that the steps overlap the procedures that we had followed for developing PBL projects (see chapter 2). We shall briefly review this process as discussed by Borg and Gall (1989; see chapter 18).

Research and Information Collecting

The research and development process begins with the assumption that a product will be developed by the researcher. During the initial stage, the researcher identifies the problem or set of issues that the product will address. It is at this stage that the student begins to think through how the product will meet a need

---

TABLE 3

Steps in the Research and Development Cycle

1. Research and information collecting
2. Planning objectives, learning activities, and small-scale testing
3. Develop preliminary form of the product
4. Preliminary field testing
5. Main product revision
6. Main field testing
7. Operational product revision
8. Operational field testing
9. Final product revision
10. Dissemination and implementation

Source: Borg and Gall (1989, pp. 784-85)

---

in the field. Borg and Gall suggest several salient questions for consideration at this point in the cycle.

1. Does the proposed product meet an important educational need?
2. Is the state of the art [in relation to the need or problem] sufficiently advanced that there is a reasonable probability that a successful product can be built?
3. Are personnel available who have the skills, knowledge, and experience necessary to build this product?
4. Can the product be developed within a reasonable period of time? (1989, p. 785)

During this stage, the student will conduct a preliminary literature review and seek to generate all information available about the problem. The student may also conduct "small-scale research," such as observations in schools and interviews with practitioners and researchers who are knowledgeable about the problem. The goal at this point is to develop a broader and deeper understanding of the problem and how it will be addressed by the product.

Planning Objectives, Learning Activities, and Small-Scale Testing

Planning of the product encompasses several of the key steps that we described in relation to PBL project development. Specifically, it is during this stage that the student develops an initial description of the product's components (for example, introduction, problem, learning objectives). Considerations of the target audience as well as the potential venue for testing also receive attention at this point. The search for literature resources that relate to the problem continues as do conversations with knowledgeable resource people.

This is also the stage during which the student develops a formal research proposal. The researcher must formulate not only a plan for development of the product, but also for its assessment. The proposal, therefore, typically includes the conventional steps of planning for data collection and analysis. While some students may have prepared a draft form of the product at this point, this is not always the case and is not a requirement. A product prospectus that delineates the nature of the problem to be addressed and the learning objectives and that suggests the direction to be taken with other features of the product is sufficient.

Development of the Preliminary Form of the Product

After project planning has been completed, the R & D process moves to the formulation of the preliminary form of the product to be tested. For our purposes, this involves the development of the problem scenario and the other facets that compose a PBL project. The outline or prospectus proposed in the previous stage is fleshed out into a fully developed prototype of the product.

Preliminary Field Test and Product Revision

"The purpose of the preliminary field test is to obtain an initial qualitative evaluation of the new educational product," write Borg and Gall (1989, p. 790). Prior to any full administration of the product, the developer should schedule a "dry run" with a group of "students" that is representative of the target audience. Critical formative feedback should be solicited in a systematic fashion. Borg and Gall caution that global ratings from participants usually overestimate the effectiveness of a product. Therefore, the design of formative-evaluation procedures should emphasize specificity in feedback.

The student uses the data obtained in the preliminary field test as the basis for preliminary product revision. This may entail revision of any or all of the product's components. Students and their professors should anticipate and plan for revision of the product at this stage. In cases where the preliminary field-test data do not suggest a need for revision, there is likely to be a flaw in the procedures used to generate the formative evaluation data. The R & D process seldom results in perfect products on the first (or second) try.

Main Field Test and Product Revision

The main field test involves implementation of the new product and collection of data concerning its application. It is at this stage that the researcher collects the key "data" concerning the new product's efficacy. Generally, the research and development process will draw heavily on evaluation designs for studying implementation of the product. As we elaborate in the next section of the chapter, the nature of the evaluation design selected varies widely. The options range from experimental designs when the primary concern is for summative assessment of outcomes to mixed quantitative and qualitative methods when the primary goal is formative evaluation of the product.

Product revision is based on the analysis of data collected during the main field test. In practice, the researcher assesses the product using both formative and summative evaluation methods. For formative purposes, the data will point to ways in which the student can improve the product. For summative purposes, the data will shed light on the efficacy of the product.

Operational Field Test and Final Product Revision

These steps require the researcher to determine "whether an educational product is fully ready for use in schools" (Borg and Gall 1989, p. 793). This will typically require the researcher to prepare others to implement the product in a variety of natural settings. The operational field test entails the collection of additional data from instructors using the product as well as student participants. These data then lead to a final revision of the product.

Dissemination, Implementation, and Institutionalization

These steps suggest the importance of making others aware of the product and enabling them to incorporate it into their educational programs. Publication of the product (for example, in a case clearinghouse), presentation of the product at professional meetings, and publication of articles about the product are several ways of disseminating information to potential users. The provision of training for trainers is an additional option for extending the use of the product.

Concluding Thoughts About the R & D Process

The R & D process involves the student in practice-oriented, systematic inquiry that leads to the development of a usable educational product. The process calls for students to synthesize content knowledge in the context of a real problem. Moreover, students must demonstrate their own understanding of the problem through the development of a product that reflects their own learning. These characteristics of the R & D model seem highly salient to the goals that we assert for Ed.D. research.

If the reader reviews chapter 2 on "Developing PBL Projects," it is apparent that our design for project development follows steps 1 through 7 of the process as delineated by Borg and Gall (see table 3). Particularly in the context of dissertation research, we do not demand that students carry out steps 8 and 9 (that is, operational field testing and product revision) of the R & D process. Students implement step 10, dissemination, at their own discretion. In the following section, we discuss how we have used the research and development process as a research model for Ed.D. students in educational administration.

Problem-Based Learning: A Model for Ed.D. Research

We present two broad options for constructing an Ed.D. dissertation around the development of a problem-based-learning project. The options are built explicitly on the research and development model. We recognize that a range of institutional interpretations exists concerning the appropriate scope of work for an Ed.D. dissertation. Therefore, we offer this discussion of options as a point of departure for others' adaptation, not as a broad prescription.

The options we present vary primarily by the nature of the research goals and the scope of the research methods employed. In option 1, the researcher poses specific research questions and draws on a traditional array of research methods to address the research questions. In option 2, a research goal (that is, development of a usable PBL project) replaces the research questions, and the investigator employs an array of research and evaluation tools to assess the PBL project. We also suggest variations on each of these broad options.

Option 1: Using a PBL Project as the Focus for Research on Problem-Based Learning

In this option, the student conducts an Ed.D. dissertation that looks quite conventional in many respects. This option involves the framing of specific research questions concerning the nature and implementation of problem-based learning as used in leadership education. The essential difference from the normal dissertation is that the research includes a set of steps that result in the development of a problem-based-learning project. Thus, the project involves the student in exploring a salient research question or set of questions in the context of implementing a self-authored PBL project.

The sources for research questions within this option are varied. They may be derived from cognitive-learning theory, literature on problem-based learning, or research on the preparation of educational leaders. Elsewhere we have discussed potential research issues that seem fruitful for study in the realm of problem-based learning (Bridges with Hallinger 1992). Research questions might focus on the effectiveness of problem-based learning when compared with traditional instruction. Alternatively, the research might explore how effective the different species of problem-based learning are in achieving the various goals of administrator-preparation programs (Bridges with Hallinger 1992, p. 112).

In this approach, the research and development model discussed above is actually embedded within a traditional research design. This option draws on Borg and Gall's notion that the R & D process has the potential to contribute to knowledge through incorporation of appropriate assessment during the main field test. As suggested by the discussion of the R & D cycle, under this option the student proceeds in three somewhat overlapping stages.

Stage 1: Problem Identification and Proposal Development

In the first stage, the student identifies research questions related to problem-based learning, reviews information salient to the research problem, identifies an important problem in practice, and develops a proposal for dissertation research. This stage incorporates the tasks delineated in the first two steps of the R & D cycle as described by Borg and Gall (see table 3).

In an Ed.D. dissertation completed at Vanderbilt, Habschmidt (1990) examined the implementation of a coauthored PBL project in the classroom. Her research was designed to explore several questions concerning problem-based learning as implemented in educational leadership programs. In framing her research questions, Habschmidt drew on an earlier paper in which Bridges (1977) analyzed the discontinuities between graduate preparation and the nature of leadership as experienced by middle managers in schools. Habschmidt's study examined the extent to which PBL, as implemented in an educational leadership class, might reduce the gap between selected features of graduate preparation in educational administration and the nature of principals' work activities.

The literature review in a research proposal under this option will typically have two sections. One section explores literature concerning the stated research problem. As noted above, the research problem of interest will arise from some combination of literatures. In Habschmidt's dissertation, this section of the literature review explored literature on problem-based learning in medical and managerial education as well as research and commentary on leadership education.

In a second section of the literature review, the student conducts a preliminary review of literature related to the focal problem that forms the basis for the PBL project. For example, at the proposal stage, Habschmidt outlined a prospectus for the development of a PBL project that would focus on the principal's role in bringing about change in a school with a stagnating culture. (This project has been published by ERIC/CEM with the title *Leadership and School Culture.*) Given the nature of the problem as presented in the field, she reviewed relevant literature on school culture, adult development, staff development, and change implementation in this portion of the proposal.

Two differences that characterize the literature-review process are worthy of mention. First, as with the classroom implementation of PBL, we encourage students to conduct a *problem-focused* review of the literature. That is, the identified problem of practice guides the student in the selection of literature for the second portion of the review. Moreover, the review is problem-focused in that we ask students to assess the literature in terms of its ability to illuminate the problem of practice.

The second distinction is that the review is not limited to the literature. Students are encouraged to seek out expertise concerning the problem wherever it may be found. Students may choose to include in their review information garnered from human resources.

The culmination of this first stage is a research proposal that outlines the research questions, presents a preliminary map of the knowledge base underlying both the research *problem* and the *project problem*, and discusses a research design for dissertation study. The research design employs methods of data collection and analysis appropriate for the study of the stated research questions.

Stage 2: Development of the PBL Project

In a second stage, the student develops, field-tests, and revises a preliminary form of the PBL project. This stage corresponds to steps 3, 4, and 5 of the research and development model outlined earlier in this chapter. The result is a full-scale prototype of the PBL project.

The student begins this process in the first stage by identifying a problem of practice and reviewing salient information. In practice, the literature review concerning the focal problem continues as the student proceeds through the project-development steps. In fact, we find that an almost continuous review of the literature is necessary. The student's very understanding of what literature is salient only becomes clear as he or she develops clarity about the problem(s) to be presented in the PBL project.

In addition, design decisions made after the problem has already been fleshed out often have implications for the types of resources needed in the project. For example, the researcher may decide relatively late in the development process on the actual form of the product specification. Completion of the product may require students to apply skills that cannot be assumed as prerequisite knowledge. In such instances, the student may need to review additional literature to identify appropriate resources for inclusion in the project.

As part of a fluid *process*, the PBL project specifications are drawn up, a preliminary field test is conducted, and the project undergoes revision based on results of the preliminary field test. After these steps, the draft project is ready for use as an *intervention* for study in the doctoral research.

Stage 3: Field Test, Data Collection and Analysis, Product Revision

In the third stage of the dissertation research, the student conducts a main field test of the PBL project. This step in the research and development process fulfills two purposes. First, during the main field test the student collects formative and summative evaluation data designed to shed light on both how the PBL project might be improved and its efficacy as an instructional tool. The formative data are derived from the same assessment techniques that we incorporate into all PBL projects (see chapters 2 and 4). The summative-evaluation techniques may go beyond those normally employed in conjunction with the project.

The student analyzes these assessment data and uses the results to inform final revision of the PBL project. This corresponds with steps 6 and 7 in the research and development process (see table 3).

Under option 1, the main field test serves the additional purpose of collecting data to answer the research questions posed for the study. This involves the collection of additional research data, which are not necessarily related to the content of the focal problem in the PBL project (for example, school culture). Rather, they are designed to illuminate the stated research questions. These data are subsequently analyzed and reported in a conventional fashion. Thus, under option 1, the final report of the study will present the data that informed final project revision as well as findings concerning the research questions.

Outcomes and Implications of Option 1 Model of a PBL Dissertation

This option for Ed.D. dissertation research has two products. First, it results in the development and publication of a field-tested problem-based-learning project. Thus far, several Vanderbilt students have completed the development of PBL projects in the context of their dissertation research. These projects are currently in use in both preservice preparation and professional-development programs in educational administration in the United States and abroad.

The second outcome of the option 1 dissertation is a contribution to research in the areas targeted by the student (that is, cognitive theory, problem-based learning, leadership education). This option holds promise for generating data that will increase our understanding of problem-based learning and its use in educational leadership preparation.

We suspect that the reader will agree that both the nature and scope of this dissertation option are substantial. In fact, the scope of option 1 exceeds the institutional norms for Ed.D. dissertations at our own institutions. As we have outlined this option, the student must conduct *at least* two full literature reviews, develop an educational intervention, and then study its implementation using conventional research methods. We would go so far as to suggest that the expectations embedded in this option meet the standards for Ph.D. study in most educational administration programs.

Given this assessment, we now note that we have presented option 1 primarily for heuristic purposes. This option suggests the outer parameters of what is possible if a student desires to use a PBL project as the focal point for dissertation research. For the purposes of an Ed.D. dissertation, however, it may be more appropriate to limit the scope of the research project.

In considering how this might be done, one possibility is for the student to substitute a previously developed PBL project for the self-authored project as a vehicle for studying features of problem-based learning in leadership education. This reduces the scope of the project considerably by eliminating all the steps involved in

PBL project development. The resulting model is akin to a conventional study of an educational intervention and would still satisfy the requirements for Ed.D. dissertations in terms of the scope and nature of the study.

We do believe that the use of PBL represents an interesting set of theoretical and empirical issues for doctoral study. However, in our judgment, it is the process of developing a PBL project in the dissertation that sets this model apart in its potential for extending the learning of the professional doctoral student. It is the development of the PBL project that we believe holds the greatest promise for transforming an Ed.D. dissertation from the frustrating exercise of "half-baked" skills into a meaningful, productive experience for professional doctoral students. Therefore, we are reluctant to see the development of the PBL project eliminated from the dissertation as a means of creating a study of manageable scope.

Development of the PBL project provides a unique opportunity for the professional doctoral student to synthesize skills, knowledge, and ways of thinking that we believe are important goals in such programs. The tasks involved in PBL project development require the student to engage in meaningful problem finding, to explore a problem of practice in depth, to draw upon salient literature and other resources that illuminate the problem, and to design a means of assisting other practitioners in learning how such a problem might be addressed in organizational settings. These are tasks that draw appropriately on the types of learning uniquely suited to the university environment and that hold practical significance in the daily work of future and current leaders.

We suggest, therefore, that the process of PBL project development itself represents an appropriate vehicle for Ed.D. research. This conclusion leads to the second option for Ed.D. dissertation research that we wish to discuss.

Option 2: Evaluation of a Problem-Based Learning Project

Given our assumptions concerning the goals of Ed.D. research, we believe that a second option exists for incorporating a PBL project into doctoral study. This option limits the goals of the dissertation to the development and evaluation of a PBL project. Rather than combining the research and development model with a conventional study of an educational intervention, the student focuses exclusively on the research and development process. We believe this option fulfills all normative expectations of an exit requirement for a professional doctorate in educational administration. In this section, we clarify how this option differs from the option presented above and elaborate on the rationale for its legitimacy as a design for Ed.D. doctoral research.

In conducting a dissertation under option 2, the student limits the scope of study to the development and evaluation of a problem-based-learning project. The student draws on the same steps indicated earlier for project development. He or she identifies a problem of practice; examines a full range of research, theory, and craft knowledge salient to the problem; and applies that knowledge in the context of developing a PBL project. This process, itself, is a variant of student-centered learning (see Bridges with Hallinger 1992, chapters 1 and 2).

The accompanying sidebar presents the components of the option 2 dissertation. These components include an introduction identifying the problem and the research goals, a review of related resources, the methodology, and a description and evaluation of the PBL project.

OPTION 2 DISSERTATION: COMPONENTS

Chapter 1: Introduction

Background

Identification of the Problem in Practice

Significance of the Problem: Why the Problem Is of Importance in Practice

Research Goals

Rationale for Developing a PBL Project for This Problem

Chapter 2: Review of Related Resources

Introduction: Knowledge Domains That Bear on the Problem

Identification and Review of Knowledge Domains: Text, Human, and Video Resources

Review of PBL Literature in Medical and Managerial Education

Synthesis of Content Issues as Related to the Problem and Use in PBL Project

Chapter 3: Methodology

General Design

Research and Development Cycle

Development of the PBL Project

Research and Information Collection

Planning (includes description of data collection and analysis)

Preliminary Development of the Product

Preliminary Field Testing (includes description of initial data collection/analysis)

Main Product Revision: Steps and Description of Revisions Made

Main Field Test: Description

Evaluation Procedures (includes main data collection/analysis for evaluation of the project)

Description of the PBL Project Developed for Implementation and Testing

Chapter 4: The PBL Project

Review of the Research Goals and General Design of the Project

Implementation of the PBL Project: Description

Evaluation Results

Summative Evaluation Results Concerning PBL Project Implementation (organize by Learning Objectives)

Formative Evaluation Results Concerning PBL Project Implementation

Other Results (optional)

Discussion of Final Product Revision (included in Appendix)

Revisions Indicated by the Formative and Summative Evaluation Results

Discussion of Classroom Implementation Issues

Problem-Finding and Identification of Research Goals

Instead of defining research questions, under option 2 the student identifies a set of research goals. These goals define the parameters of the student's study. The incorporation of *research goals* rather than *research questions* explicitly indicates that the researcher is not setting out to answer a set of research questions. The proposed outcome of the study is a product—the creation of a PBL project that has been evaluated—not a set of research findings. Thus, it is here where the scope of the project is reduced and the dissertation departs from conventional Ed.D. and Ph.D. models.

Jennings (1992) conducted an Ed.D. dissertation consistent with this model. The first step in the process involved identification of a focal problem for his dissertation. The focal problem he selected concerned the problem of high rates of academic failure for poor children in urban elementary schools. As an associate superintendent in an urban school system, he saw first-hand not only the scope of the problem at the elementary level, but also the consequences for students and the rest of the school system.

Thus, Jennings' dissertation focused on a real problem faced in his and other urban school systems. His research goals involved the development of a PBL project that would help urban elementary principals respond to this problem. His PBL project sought to engage school principals in learning about (1) the effectiveness of early intervention with at-risk students, (2) the nature of research-based early intervention programs available to principals, and (3) how a knowledge of change theory might inform the implementation of an early intervention program in a school. The goal of the dissertation would be reflected in its outcome: a fully developed PBL project on early intervention.

Synthesizing the Literature

At the proposal stage, we still ask students to conduct a full review of the literature on problem-based learning as it has evolved in various fields. This review of the literature is conducted despite the fact that it will not lead to the identification of a researchable problem as it does in option 1. PBL represents the primary vehicle for the student's research and development project. Therefore, it is essential that he or she demonstrate an indepth understanding of the instructional methodology and the options for employing it in the course of the dissertation study.

Although the Ed.D. study may not be exploring an explicit research question, we still encourage students to use the dissertation as an informal opportunity for systematic innovation in the use of problem-based learning. For example, one of our students is currently exploring the adaptation of a concept used widely in problem-based medical education: "the standardized patient" (see Barrows 1985, chapter 2, Appendix II). This involves thinking through issues concerned with adapting PBL to leadership education and including some means of assessing the results, even if only in a formative manner. The results of this *informal experimentation* can be presented in the final report of the dissertation.

As in option 1, the student will also review literature in the knowledge domains salient to the focal problem for the PBL project. It is in the nature of PBL-oriented literature reviews that they take the student into interdisciplinary domains. For his study, Jennings (1992) reviewed research on effective schools, early intervention programs, school law, leadership, change, learning theory, and educational equity.

As we noted earlier, the process of PBL project development involves the student in an iterative process of problem-finding and exploration. Thus, Jennings' conception of the original problem and how it might be addressed evolved through the process of reviewing the research literature as it applied to the problem he had identified. The research review for his proposal actually took him into knowledge domains that were not included later in the dissertation itself. The evolutionary process that unfolds in PBL project development may be viewed as an indicator of the student's engagement in a meaningful synthesis of the literature.

In discussions with colleagues, it is clear that the literature review associated with Ed.D. dissertations is a task that normally causes untold frustration for both students and faculty. Yet, as with PBL in the classroom, our doctoral students find that reviewing the literature in light of a real problem that has meaning for them in practice changes the very nature of their reading of the literature. Moreover, we find that students do not object to the extra work involved in the interdisciplinary literature review, since it is both meaningful to them and they are making the decisions as to what is relevant to understanding the problem they have chosen to explore.

Developing the PBL Module

At the proposal stage, as in option 1, the student follows the preliminary literature review with an outline of the steps to be taken in the development of the PBL project. These steps follow those detailed in chapter 2. They outline the roadmap the student will follow in the development, field testing, and evaluation of the PBL project.

At this stage in the proposal process, the student may propose the nature of the problematic situation to be used in the project and formulate a set of tentative learning objectives. In addition, considerable attention in this portion of the research proposal must be paid to the techniques to be used in assessing the PBL project. Even though this dissertation model does not incorporate research questions, the student is still expected to develop and implement a systematic plan for assessing the PBL project.

Evaluating the PBL Project

A plan must be included in the research proposal that outlines both data collection and analysis strategies to be used in assessing the project. There are two major variations that we have considered in relation to evaluation of the PBL project within the context of an Ed.D. dissertation. The variation hinges on the extent to which the plan for evaluating the PBL project goes beyond the normal assessment steps of project development in summative evaluation.

As we have discussed at length elsewhere in this volume, the emphasis in assessment for PBL projects is on formative evaluation. The purpose of this formative evaluation is to generate useful feedback for students' learning and for the instructor's improvement of the project materials. The formative evaluation techniques typically include "Talk Back" sheets, integrative essays, work products, and instructor observations.

These sources of data complement more limited forms of summative evaluation with which we have experimented in implementing PBL. These include knowledge-review exercises of various sorts as well as the work products of students.

In planning for the evaluation of a PBL project in the context of an Ed.D. dissertation under option 2, the student and advisor must determine the appropriate scope of the assessment. If the goal of the evaluation is to produce a PBL project that meets the standards we have recommended in this volume, then the normal complement of formative and summative assessment tools would seem appropriate.

In other cases, institutional expectations for the Ed.D. dissertation as an exit requirement may demand additional demonstration of proficiency in research methods. Then the normal battery of formative and summative assessment techniques may be supplemented with additional summative measures of student learning. In this case, the student will formulate an assessment strategy that seeks to measure what participants have learned from the PBL module.

This can be accomplished by linking formal summative measures explicitly to the project's learning objectives. These measures will generate data for the final report on what students learned. This information will complement the discussion of results from the analysis of the formative evaluation data and how these were used to revise the PBL project.

Assessment of the PBL Dissertation

Criteria for assessing the student's research project also deserve at least brief attention in this context. The defining characteristic of this dissertation model is its focus on the development of linkages among research, theory, and practice. Thus, we believe that this should also become the focal point for assessment of the student's dissertation.

This focus on linking research, theory, and practice has two implications. First, it may be appropriate for faculty members to adjust their expectations concerning the extensiveness and sophistication of procedures for data collection and analysis. The project has as its goal the creation of a PBL project with a high degree of face and content validity. The evaluation procedures for the project need primarily to establish that the project meets high standards in those domains. This may not necessarily require the types of advanced research tools asked of Ph.D. students.

We are not suggesting that the faculty's standards for the project are reduced. Nor do we mean to imply that students are given greater leeway in the procedures to be followed in project development. Our admonition to faculty is only that assessment of the PBL-oriented dissertation should reflect the nature of the project's goals.

Second, and leading from our first point, the assessment of the student's project should focus primarily on the degree to which the student has achieved a reasonable synthesis of research, theory, and practice in the product. Some criteria for assessing the project emerge naturally from this perspective. Relevant questions might include:

1. Is the problem addressed in the project important in practice? Is this clearly established in the project's introduction, with supporting data provided in the body of the dissertation?

2. Does the problem's representation in the project specifications reflect the complexity of the workplace?

3. Is there a strong linkage between the problem as it is presented and the learning objectives stated in the project specifications?

4. Are the resources selected for inclusion in the project applicable to the problem? Do they reflect the state of the art of research, theory, and practical wisdom concerning the problems presented in the project? Is there evidence that students found them useful in understanding and solving the problem(s) during the field test?

5. Do the performance product(s) in the project engage the students in a valid form of managerial work activity? Is the nature of the product(s) consistent with the form of workplace resolution for similar problems? Do the types of work products incorporated into the project stimulate students to draw on the resources provided? Are students stimulated to engage human as well as text resources? Do the actual products developed by students during the main field test reflect high-quality efforts to address the problem within the constraints of classroom training?

6. Do the formative-assessment techniques in the PBL project provide the desired range of feedback for the instructor? Do the summative-evaluation techniques incorporated into the dissertation, as well as those included in the PBL project, provide sufficient data for their respective purposes? Does the evaluation reflect input concerning the project's efficacy from the perspectives of practice and research-based inquiry? Has the student maintained high standards in carrying out the evaluation and revision of the project? Are the steps followed clearly described and replicable?

7. Is the linkage among components of the PBL project clearly in evidence? Have gaps or weak linkages in the PBL project been identified and adequately addressed in the course of project development?

This focus on practice has an additional implication, not for assessment criteria, but for who makes the assessment. Clive Dimmock, a colleague at the University of Western Australia, has observed that since the goal of this dissertation is to contribute to practice, practitioners should be included on the assessment committee. In chapter 2, we noted that we often ask practitioners to react to the performance product that emerges from the product specifications through participation in a role play. Consistent with Professor Dimmock's observation, we also systematically include on the dissertation committee a respected practitioner with demonstrated expertise in the problem domain of the PBL project. We have found that having a practitioner on the committee helps maintain the doctoral student's focus on the reality of the problem throughout the dissertation. It also provides an important perspective at the point of assessing the dissertation.

We acknowledge that asking practitioners to serve on dissertation committees is not, in and of itself, an innovation. This is standard practice in educational administration programs at any number of institutions. However, many practitioners serve on dissertation committees as second-class citizens, deferring to the professors on most, if not all, matters. Despite holding doctoral degrees themselves, they may feel less qualified to judge either the process or outcomes of the doctoral student's research (an outcome of their own dissertation experience?).

Therefore, their role on the dissertation committee often takes on a ritualistic character with few substantive contributions emerging from their participation. Thus far, our experience suggests that practitioners serve more actively and make a more meaningful contribution to the PBL-oriented dissertation. Observing their participation in several instances, they more readily express opinions and form judgments concerning the quality of the student's product.

From our perspective, the student's PBL project (and discussion of the project's development) represents a concrete demonstration of the "bridge" the student has constructed connecting research and theory to practice. Since the nature of this bridge is evident in the products that result from the dissertation (for example, the PBL project, the work products from the main field test), we can actually raise our standards for professional students. Instead of applying the standards used for the Ph.D., we apply standards that fit the type of degree, our goals for the student, and the nature of the dissertation.

The criteria outlined above address the extent to which the student has identified a significant problem in practice and used both tools of the academy and professional practice to illuminate it. The assessment focuses on the student's ability to use tools of systematic inquiry toward a practical end. The inclusion of practitioners during the project and, as significantly, in assessment of the dissertation products rounds out the practice-oriented focus of this Ed.D. dissertation process.

Concluding Thoughts on the Role of Problem-Based Learning in the Ed.D. Dissertation

The Ed.D. dissertation represents the object of our greatest aspirations for professional doctoral students in educational administration. As professors, we hope this research project—the nature of which was defined for quite different academic purposes—will provide a vehicle for our students to demonstrate enhanced capacities for inquiry and reflection. Unfortunately, it has been our experience that too few of our professional students reach this goal. More often, they labor to satisfy a formal set of academically derived requirements without understanding the relevance of research and inquiry to their current or future work roles. In this final section, we briefly discuss the outcomes of working with professional doctoral students on PBL-oriented dissertations.

Outcomes of the PBL Research Process

The sample of students whom we have mentored in the fashion described is still small. However, students who have developed PBL projects in the course of their doctoral research have had such personally and professionally productive experiences that we chose to elaborate on them. Moreover, as faculty mentors, we have both experienced benefits for ourselves and have observed benefits for the profession.

Benefits for Students

Students report that the process of developing and evaluating a PBL project has several tangible benefits for them. The process naturally leads students—some for the first time—to make meaningful connections across courses in their doctoral program. The R & D process requires them to integrate content from different disciplines and forces them to assess the research literature in light of problems of practice. Again, this leads students to take on a more critical perspective when reviewing the literature, the absence of which professors commonly bemoan.

The R & D cycle also calls on students to employ inquiry skills and research tools, but for a purpose that they view as practically relevant. During the process of PBL project development, the student engages in systematic and extended problem-finding and problem-solving. The convergence of these in the process of developing a usable PBL project also validates students' experience as practitioners.

Surprisingly, these capacities are not always developed or applied in the context of Ed.D. dissertations. Thus, when conducted with care, this form of dissertation provides a vehicle for students to synthesize desirable knowledge, inquiry skills, and ways of thinking that are highly relevant to practitioners. These outcomes reflect the type of higher order thinking processes that we want our professional doctoral students to develop.

Our students who have incorporated PBL into their Ed.D. dissertations identify another benefit from this approach. They note that the process facilitates their transition from "graduate school" back into the workplace (whether or not they ever left!). This results from three related factors inherent in the PBL process. First, the process engages students in the active integration of craft knowledge gained from their past experience with the new knowledge and skills gained through advanced training. Second, the process allows students to demonstrate that they have learned something that is academically respectable and practically relevant. Third, the process results in the creation of a product, the PBL project, that is explicitly designed for use by others in the field. Much as the Ph.D. does for future researchers, these features of the PBL research process provide an opportunity for Ed.D. students to practice skills and ways of thinking that will have normative and instrumental value to them as administrators as they advance in their careers.

These outcomes reinforce the notion that the student has accomplished something uniquely suited to his or her status as a practitioner who has succeeded in advanced study. Ed.D. graduates, who may previously have felt like second-rate Ph.D. researchers, instead manifest a well-earned sense of professional pride and satisfaction. There is no condescension or poor-cousin comparison to the work of Ph.D. peers in their program. On the contrary, the Ed.D. students have developed a product that draws upon their particular skills in a way that Ph.D. students, lacking similar professional experience, would have difficulty duplicating! To the extent that this occurs, we believe that the Ed.D. dissertation has served a useful purpose.

Benefits for Professors

The options that we have presented here also have potentially positive benefits for the professors who mentor such projects. Our experience in working with students on the development of PBL projects places us in a very different, and healthier, role vis a vis students. Within the context of these research projects, our students are able to contribute information concerning educational problems derived from their experience as practitioners. The results in terms of problem identification and description are beyond anything we could contribute from our distanced perspective in the university.

At the same time, as faculty mentors we are able to assist students by applying a more broadly focused lens to the particular problems they encounter in the workplace. We also assist by guiding them through a systematic process of inquiry into the selected problems that are salient to them. This inquiry process draws on the tools of the academy, but in a practice-focused fashion. This creates a more balanced and productive professional relationship between the professor and the professional doctoral student, a relationship that honors the expertise that each has to offer.

These features of the PBL research process are also beneficial to faculty in that they challenge us to maintain an active connection to the field. The process of mentoring students in these PBL projects helps us keep the tools of our craft sharpened through continuous application to problems of practice. This can begin to reshape how the professor looks at knowledge and inquiry in the field of educational administration. It reminds us that as professors in a professional field, we have an ongoing commitment to address the problems of the field as well as our academic interests.

Benefits to the Profession

Finally, this route also holds the potential of generating tangible benefits to the profession. The highly circumscribed contribution of knowledge either to research or practice by Ed.D. dissertations is no secret within the profession. Given the large numbers of professional doctoral students, we believe this is a cause for concern within the profession. Does the expenditure of student and faculty resources justify the results that emerge from the Ed.D. dissertation process?

Our experience thus far bears out the conclusion that the options presented here have significant potential for generating high-quality materials that can be used in educational administration programs. The projects developed through this process are already being used in training programs in several countries (for example, U.S., Canada, Australia, New Zealand, Thailand, England, Israel).

Given the high front-end costs of developing PBL materials, this is an encouraging finding as we consider the challenges of curriculum implementation. The adoption of these materials by professors and professional trainers provides additional testimony to the quality of the products that emerge from the inquiry process described in this chapter.

We note further that the PBL projects produced to date through Ed.D. dissertation research have been created by doctoral students attending Vanderbilt's weekend, offcampus program in educational leadership. Although these are able students, the program is subject to as many, if not more, academic constraints than many other doctoral programs. This gives us confidence that students in other Ed.D. programs can develop products of similarly high quality.

In addition to generating materials for the educational administration curriculum, this dissertation process has an additional potential benefit for the profession. We sense that the students who emerge from this experience leave their programs with a healthier respect for the university and its role in professional practice. Since these graduates represent our lifeline to the field, this bodes well for maintaining the vitality of our programs.

Conclusion

In this chapter, we have sought to go beyond the criticism that is commonly aimed at the Ed.D. degree by offering an alternative route for students at the dissertation stage. We believe that the options for using PBL project development as a focus for Ed.D. dissertations hold significant promise for the field. This belief is grounded in the benefits that we have observed for our students and that we have experienced as professors. It is our assessment that these models represent viable, academically sound, and practically relevant vehicles for professional doctoral research.

We encourage our colleagues to use this discussion as the point of departure for their own experimentation. There are, undoubtedly, other permutations of this general approach that have not occurred to us. We would welcome hearing about extensions and adaptations of the models we have proposed here. We close this chapter with a reflection from a doctoral student who summed up her experience of using this approach in Ed.D. research.

The idea to try and create something usable out of what I had learned in my coursework was more than a challenge. It was a chance to engage my creativity after a long period of responding primarily to the expectations of professors in my courses. I looked forward to the opportunity to be innovative and pull together what I knew from my experience with what I had learned in courses. . . .

The project entailed more work than I ever expected from having been a participant in PBL projects during class. My project kept growing! *Even after the scope of the project seemed to have been bounded through the format of the project specifications, it kept growing in depth.* The more I looked at the problem and explored it, the more alternatives became apparent. That became the new challenge; not only understanding the issues myself, but formulating the project in a way that others could gain that knowledge in a meaningful but less time-consuming fashion.

Looking back, I learned that it's definitely easier to start a PBL project than to finish one. It's also not as easy as it looks to teach with one. Field testing and systematic assessment, which seemed like after-thoughts at first, became meaningful when I actually reached those stages in the development process.... Doing this project helped reveal how much I had known from my experience, how much I had learned, and how much more there was to learn.

6

Implementing Problem-Based Learning: Issues in Curricular and Instructional Change

Prior to becoming a school teacher and administrator, Hallinger worked as a cabinetmaker.

Quite a few years ago, before my career in education, I had decided to become a cabinetmaker. The traditional approach to learning this trade is through an extended apprenticeship. Accordingly, I went in search of a master cabinetmaker from whom I could learn the craft. After several unsuccessful attempts to contact one particular cabinetmaker by phone, I drove down to the address given for his shop. Standing in front of the shop was a man who looked to be in his seventies wearing a blue denim apron with the inscription, *Karl from East Berlin*. He was leaning on a broom, chatting with passersby. I approached him hesitantly and asked, "Is there any chance that you might be looking for someone to help out in your shop?"

He replied: "So you want to be a cabinetmaker? What makes you think you can be a cabinetmaker? You can't learn this craft from a book. No! It's not something you can learn from the TV. No! You can't pick the knowledge out of the air. No! Experience! Experience is the only way to learn this trade. Me, I have 65 years of experience—Germany, Argentina, the United States—apprenticed with a master cabinetmaker in Berlin for four years, 1912 to 1916, before the Kaiser called me. . . . So, you think that you want to be a cabinetmaker? Let me see your hands. Hmm. . . . Do you think that you can sweep leaves off a roof?"

This story illustrates the longer tradition within which problem-based learning exists. This is the tradition of learning from doing. Embedded in Karl's litany is the belief that knowledge of cabinetmaking must be learned at the point where it is applied. The apprenticeship model represents a system that provides experience but also supports the ability of the novice to learn from mistakes. Try to imagine learning cabinetmaking solely through books or the TV.

Before we can say that we have "learned" something, we must undergo a process of taking knowledge derived both from our new experiences and the experience of others and making it part of our own patterns of thinking and doing. This process involves developing an understanding of the formal meaning of the information, reconsidering past beliefs in light of the new information, and constructing a new viewpoint.

We contend that PBL incorporates important features of a similar process of learning from one's experience. Some have referred to this as a "cognitive apprenticeship." The cognitive apprenticeship enables the students to learn skills, ways of thinking about one's role, and the norms of the profession. Karl's final question, "Can you sweep leaves off the roof?," was not a question about skill, but actually foreshadowed initial entry into the status of apprentice.

Throughout this volume, we have sought to convey how problem-based learning serves to fulfill these instrumental and normative functions. As Barrows and Tamblyn (1980) have observed, the principles that underlie PBL follow what we might call a *natural* process of learning.

> We read journals and attend conferences and seminars to stay current in our fields; yet most of the information is soon forgotten. If we run into a difficult case or problem, however, and have to read, consult colleagues and experts for advice, or research the literature for help, the information we gain invariably is far better retained. (p. 17)

We have designed the version of PBL discussed in this volume to build on this simple observation. The design of PBL projects, the form of teaching in the classroom, the organization of the curriculum, and the methods of assessment create a mutually reinforcing learning environment. This learning environment allows students to obtain new knowledge in light of experience generated by the PBL problems. Tradition, current theory, and empirical research suggest that this process leads to learning that can be applied to the real problems students encounter outside the classroom.

In prior chapters, we examined specific issues that pertain to the implementation of PBL. Here we wish to consider the change process that unfolds as we introduce PBL as an instructional and curricular innovation. We organize the discussion around a number of challenges that arise when seeking to make the transition to PBL. For each of these potential obstacles, we describe the various strategies that we have used.

Throughout this book, we have claimed that PBL represents a radical departure from traditional forms of learning in higher education. As an instructional and curricular innovation, the implementation of PBL is subject to numerous obstacles. Scholars frequently conceive of the change process in three overlapping stages: adoption, implementation, and institutionalization (Berman and McLaughlin 1978, Fullan 1991, Hall and Hord 1987). We review the challenges associated with each of these stages and discuss how they might be addressed by change agents. A *change agent* is anyone who assumes responsibility for initiating or stimulating others to use PBL in an instructional setting.

Adoption Stage: Challenges and Change Strategies

During this stage of the change process, change agents must raise the awareness of people concerning the innovation and interest them in its potential use. There is no reason to assume that most instructors, either in the university or staff development settings, will necessarily see a reason to change their way of teaching. In chapter 3, we included an excerpt from an essay in which an undergraduate student reflects on the fairly dramatic change that she experienced in the transition to a PBL environment. As we elaborate in that same chapter, the change in role behaviors is at least as great for teachers who attempt to use PBL as for students.

In higher education institutions, instruction receives a relatively low priority. Given this fact of academic life, why should faculty take on a radical innovation that will require considerable front-end learning and preparation? How could one stimulate colleagues to experiment with this innovation?

Why Change?

In addressing the first of these two questions, we can reflect on how the adoption of PBL has influenced us as faculty members. PBL has resulted in numerous benefits for us, many of which we have noted in preceding chapters:

- Healthier relationships between faculty and students

- More balanced relationships with practitioners

- Broader and deeper familiarity with significant problems of practice

- Sharpened awareness of how our empirical research and conceptual analyses relate to practice

- More productive practice-focused research with professional doctoral students

- More positive responses from students concerning the outcomes of their learning

- More demonstrable, steeper growth in students' cognitive and affective capacities for group leadership

- Greater insight into both what and how students are learning

- Renewal and reinforcement of the fundamental belief that as instructors we do have something of substance to contribute to the improvement of professional practice

Among the benefits that we have listed here, we want to place special emphasis on those that concern the student. It is a characteristic of innovation in the professional practices of teachers that they are most strongly influenced to change when they clearly perceive tangible benefits for their students (Fullan 1991, Hall and Hord

1987). Thus, observations of students' responses and data generated by students represent the most important information for teachers when considering the adoption of PBL.

At our own institutions, we have used four practical strategies for informing and stimulating teachers to consider the use of PBL in the classroom. The reader should note that these strategies do not assume prior knowledge or interest on the part of the staff.

Change strategy no. 1: Use faculty as expert consultants

One strategy we have used has been to ask faculty colleagues to participate in PBL projects as expert consultants. This takes two forms: consultation in project development and active participation as consultants during the project.

In the first instance, we seek assistance from colleagues concerning their expertise in specific knowledge domains when developing PBL projects. As described in chapter 2, we actively seek out perspectives from a variety of disciplines to ensure that we are broadening students' understanding of educational problems by providing a rich set of interdisciplinary resources. These consultations have sparked colleagues' interest in PBL through reading the problems and considering how their domain of expertise might bear upon it. Our discussions with these colleagues have often ranged further into how PBL works both conceptually and practically.

As expert consultants during the project, the faculty members participate in first-hand dialogue with students on the content of PBL projects in which the instructors have expertise. We offered guidelines for this role in the chapter on classroom implementation. Invariably these direct observations impress faculty with the seriousness of students' involvement in the project. The discussions between faculty and students reflect the students' active engagement of the curricular content and answer many questions faculty have concerning the nature of conceptual development in a PBL environment.

Both of these roles demystify the PBL process for faculty members and allow them to test the waters in a nonthreatening way. They begin to learn about what PBL is and how it works in the classroom. They can see PBL materials first-hand and experience aspects of the PBL process. These are keys to stimulating interest in instructional innovations (Hall and Hord 1987).

Change strategy no. 2: Involve faculty as panelists during PBL projects

A second way of introducing faculty members to PBL is to use them as panelists in PBL projects. These naturally occurring events can be leveraged to inform and interest colleagues in the use of PBL. We note two ways in which faculty members participate as panelists.

The first case is where the role being played in the PBL project is one of a university faculty member. Propitiously, this role occurs in the introductory project that we use with students, *Because Wisdom Cannot Be Told* (see Appendix A).

This project scenario presents students with problems of increasing student dissatisfaction with instruction and declining enrollment in a higher education department that serves professional students. The department faces substantial budget cuts if it does not come up with a reasonable plan to address the problem. The project places students in the role of professors serving on a faculty subcommittee that has been charged with exploring PBL as one instructional alternative for departmental consideration. The outcome of the project is for students to make a presentation to the full department's faculty concerning what they learned about PBL that is relevant to the department's problem. Then they must make a recommendation concerning its adoption by the department and offer a supporting rationale.

This project represents a unique opportunity not only to introduce our students to PBL, but also to convey the results of their study to faculty! Each time we use the project, we solicit different faculty members in our own department to role-play the faculty at the ensuing department meeting. The students, role-playing the committee members, make their presentation concerning what PBL is, the research on its efficacy, and how it operates in the classroom. Then they make a recommendation concerning adoption by the department. The fact that our faculty colleagues are truly naive about PBL not only comes as somewhat of a surprise to the students, but also adds to the "reality" of the situation.

This vehicle builds our own faculty's awareness concerning PBL. It provides faculty members with a succinct, informative presentation on the nature of PBL and its efficacy as derived from theory, empirical research, and the students' own experience of PBL during the project. As a change strategy, it also conveys the students' perspectives toward problem-based learning and their ultimate recommendation concerning its use. Notably, these are the same students taught by the panelists in other courses.

The second type of panel participation occurs when faculty colleagues assist us by assuming a role other than that of university faculty (for example, superintendent, school board member) during a project performance. Whenever possible we seek *real practitioners* who occupy the role being assumed in the project to engage in panels and other role-plays. There are, however, times when we need an extra pair of hands to assist in a project role. This may occur when there is a large class and we must set up more than one role-play setting. In situations like this, we ask faculty colleagues to assume the practitioner role.

The nature of this role-play differs somewhat from the one previously described. Since such projects focus on the substance of school administration rather than on PBL, participation does not provide the same type of information to the faculty member(s) about PBL. Nonetheless, as a panelist in the role-play, the professor is able to observe in a realistic setting the nature of students' engagement in PBL.

The timing of this interaction in the project process is significant. Participation at the conclusion of a project allows faculty members to form first-hand impressions of the students' understanding of the project's curriculum content at a salient moment. Although not intended for this purpose, direct observation of students begins to answer faculty members' questions about how well they learn the course content through the PBL approach.

Change strategy no. 3: Use naturally occurring campus events as opportunities to discuss PBL with faculty and students

At our institutions, the faculty-student bag lunch is a common occurrence. We have used this and other naturally occurring events (for example, topical presentation, guest lectures) as a means of informing colleagues and students about PBL. Given the limited time available in these settings, we set a goal of stimulating interest in PBL. We may provide a short lecture, present an illustrative project problem, share sample materials and student products, and ask a student who has participated in PBL to assist us in answering questions. Again, the presence of students gives faculty members an initial opportunity to gauge their interest in this method of learning.

Change strategy no. 4: Share student products with faculty

We have found that our colleagues are interested in several types of student products that evolve naturally from PBL. As a result of seeing our colleagues' positive reaction, we have begun to be more systematic in sharing selected products with them. This has turned out to be a useful means of raising our colleagues' awareness of PBL and interesting them in potential adoption.

The first type of product is represented by the actual work products generated by students in a PBL project. None of our colleagues is interested in reading additional batches of student papers. We do, however, find them to be interested in viewing products that demonstrate students' ability to bridge research and practice. These may be written products such as a memo, a strategic plan, or a teacher-evaluation report.

Surprisingly, our colleagues have also been interested in reading selected integrative essays written by students. These essays provide quite direct insight into students' thinking about the content of the course and PBL. Written in plain, direct language, the essays express the nature of the students' engagement in the course.

As we have already suggested, an additional product of interest to faculty is the project performance. Thus, at times we invite their participation in, or observation of, a product performance. A videotaped excerpt of students engaged in PBL may also be shared as a stimulus during a discussion on PBL, for example, during a bag lunch.

Reflections on Adoption of PBL

We cannot claim tactical brilliance for the development of these strategies. Our experience is actually fully consistent with Fullan's (1991) observations concerning the evolutionary nature of change implementation. These strategies evolved out of our own practical needs for collegial assistance during our personal implementation of PBL. Notably, it has not been our intention to *sell* our colleagues on the virtues of PBL. Perhaps, because our need was as real as the instructional settings in which our colleagues observed PBL in use, their response has been overwhelmingly positive.

These strategies have, over time, begun to inform and interest other faculty in the adoption of PBL. At Vanderbilt, four other colleagues in the Department of Educational Leadership have chosen to experiment with PBL in their teaching. In two courses, Social Context of Education and Higher Education Administration, colleagues have worked with their students on project development with interesting results. Another professor has adapted a simulation he had developed previously for use in a PBL format. At Stanford, a colleague in the Psychological Studies in Education department has been using PBL as the main instructional strategy in the Health Psychology in Education program.

It was never our intention to use PBL in undergraduate education. However, Hallinger's assignment to teach in Peabody College's undergraduate leadership education program has provided an unanticipated opportunity to experiment with PBL in this setting. Professors in this program often feel acutely the constraints of working with students who lack a basis in experience for many of the issues addressed in the curriculum. The results of using PBL with these students have been encouraging, particularly from the students' perspective. Consequently, other professors are beginning to seek us out for more information on how to incorporate PBL into the undergraduate leadership-education curriculum.

Implementation Stage: Challenges and Change Strategies

At the implementation stage, interested faculty must develop the skills needed to use the educational innovation in their settings.

This conceptualization of the change process assumes that awareness and interest represent necessary but insufficient conditions to
bring about actual use of an innovation. Systematic faculty development as well as collegial and logistical support weigh heavily in
determining the actual success of implementation. Here we focus
on two specific challenges: (1) understanding the PBL methodology and (2) providing resource support.

At this stage, instructors need to develop a more complete
understanding of PBL and how it works prior to implementation.
Research on change implementation finds that *mutual adaptation* is
a natural part of the change process (Fullan and Pomfret 1977,
McLaughlin and others 1978). That is, successful implementation
often involves adaptation of the innovation to meet the needs of the
particular setting. This applies to instructional techniques and curriculum materials as well as policies (Fullan 1991).

'I Already Use PBL in My Teaching'

There is a risk, however, that excessive adaptation will under-
mine fidelity to the fundamental principles that underlie an innovation. Therefore, those responsible for implementation must first
be knowledgeable about and skilled in the use of the innovation
before making decisions concerning adaptation (Berman and
McLaughlin 1978, Joyce and Showers 1983). Research conducted
by Hall and Hord (1987) concludes that individuals tend to react
out of concerns for personal and task competence early in the
change process. When confronted with an innovation, potential
users have a propensity to reduce complexity and cognitive disso-
nance by absorbing the unknown into the familiar. Thus, the implementation stage is not the appropriate time for users to make
significant changes in the design of an innovation.

Our own experience in working with professors on the implementation of PBL bears out this conclusion. In the training sessions
that we have conducted on PBL, participants often have come with
the firm belief that they are already using PBL in their classes. Their
personal conception of PBL may reflect experiences with case teaching. In other instances, the teacher may present a problem as the
stimulus for student discussion in small groups.

While both of these techniques include features of PBL, they do not begin to approximate PBL as we have described it in this volume. These surface similarities do, however, represent a challenge for implementation. This issue is particularly salient because of the multifaceted, mutually reinforcing design of PBL. As noted earlier, to achieve consistency in learning, the various elements that comprise PBL must work in concert.

Experience in using problem-based approaches in medical education bears this out. After reviewing different PBL approaches that had evolved in medical education, Barrows concluded that only one variant could be expected to contribute *optimally* to students' achievement (Barrows 1986). The other models sacrifice one or more of the important elements that provide power to the learning model.

During our own process of adapting PBL for leadership education, the method has undergone numerous transmutations. We remain eclectic in our own implementation of PBL. The wide range of contexts in which we have used PBL demands this. We are, however, quite cautious and carefully consider the implications for each change that we contemplate in the basic design when adapting PBL. We urge other users of PBL to exercise similar caution and care when implementing PBL.

Use of PBL To Instruct Professors in PBL

We have already described in some detail the philosophy and selected content of training we provide to instructors in PBL (see chapter 3). Here we remind the reader that gaining expertise through the actual use of PBL is a highly cost-effective strategy. Using PBL as the means of accomplishing this training increases confidence in the instructor's ability to use the method and also demonstrates the amount and nature of the learning that results from the process.

In training sessions, we take pains to clarify in a direct fashion the distinctions between PBL and case teaching. Our experience indicates, however, that faculty members must actually participate in one or more projects before they obtain a truly meaningful understanding of how the different elements that comprise PBL function in a mutually reinforcing manner. This understanding is essential.

Resource Support for Implementation

A second major concern at the implementation stage is the provision of adequate resources to support training and experimentation. In the context of PBL, resources are needed for training, curriculum development, and classroom implementation. Without adequate resources, it is difficult to achieve successful implementation of PBL. We suggest several strategies for addressing each of these challenges to successful implementation.

Change strategy no. 1: Use existing materials to support implementation

This strategy to address the resource issue begins by suggesting the use of materials offered in this book as well as those available commercially and through the authors as the basis for training and the curriculum. Although we periodically offer training institutes in PBL, the *Because Wisdom Cannot Be Told* project that we use to introduce students to PBL can also be used by professors to learn about PBL. An individual or a small group of professors could use this PBL project in self-directed study to learn the basics of PBL.

Change strategy no. 2: Use faculty research projects to generate curriculum materials

Ongoing research conducted by faculty can generate curriculum materials in a cost-effective manner. The professor can draw upon data collected through ongoing research projects as the basis for a PBL project. This brings the research to life and enhances its utility for practitioners.

We offer three examples. First, Hallinger constructed one PBL project, *Jump Starting Educational Reform: The Role of the Superintendent in School Restructuring*, around case study data collected in a restructuring school district. This project evolved as the researcher was actively working with the superintendent of the district in understanding the obstacles that were impeding reform in the district. The process of project development engaged the researcher in seeking out help in the literature for a very practical and significant problem faced by the superintendent and his team of administrators.

In a second example, Hallinger worked with a colleague, Joseph Murphy, in developing a PBL project around data collected in their research on curriculum inequity. This project, *Is Everyone Learning? Assessing and Improving Student Opportunity to Learn in Secondary Schools*, presents a problem scenario built around nonequal access to learning in a secondary school. The project uses sanitized student transcripts that were drawn from an actual research study. Students must analyze these transcripts, much as the researchers did, to reveal students' opportunities to learn that are shaped by the school's curriculum policies.

In a third example, Bridges crafted a PBL project around a set of documents that he gathered during a five-year study of how school administrators deal with incompetent teachers. This project, *Dealing with Problem Teachers*, contains a number of problems that are based on a personnel file of an incompetent teacher. This file contains copies of classroom observations, annual evaluations of the teacher, and assistance plans. All these were prepared by the supervising principal. The learning resources that accompany this project were also identified by Bridges as part of the literature review he conducted during the life of his research study. This project seeks to develop knowledge about the legal aspects of teacher evaluation. It also promotes skills in preparing defensible documentation and in developing remediation plans that are consistent with research findings on the effectiveness of inservice training.

In each of these instances, the project-development process not only resulted in a PBL project, but also deepened the researchers' understanding of the problem under investigation. Moreover, for the purposes of the present discussion, the freshness of the data and the access to relevant information reduced the time needed for project development considerably.

Change strategy no. 3: Use student research projects to generate curriculum materials

As we outlined in chapter 5, dissertation projects conducted by our professional students represent a potential gold mine of opportunities for materials development. Systematic attention to the nature of the problems around which students create their projects could, over time, contribute to the development of a course or curriculum by an instructor or a department. These materials could be tailor made to the regional context in which the university operates.

For example, the state of Kentucky has adopted a set of state-wide policies governing the implementation of school-based management and shared decision-making in K-12 schools. It is conceivable that an educational administration department could undertake to systematically develop, through its doctoral students, PBL projects that address the significant common problems that administrators face in this particular policy and cultural context. Additional projects could be developed over time as the problems and knowledge base evolve.

A less complete, but still viable, variation on this strategy is to use projects developed as class projects as the basis for materials that professors codevelop with students. At Vanderbilt, Hallinger teaches a course on Integrated Inquiry in which each student develops a preliminary draft of a PBL project. These drafts are of sufficient quality that a professor could decide to continue working with the student through additional steps of the project-development cycle.

Change strategy no. 4: Develop a system of collegial support

We have personally found this strategy to be critical in our own experimentation with PBL. It is possible, as we can attest, to develop a shared system of support even with colleagues who are not at your own institution. We exchange project materials, discuss problems by phone and e-mail, and share student products. This collegial support enriches our teaching and learning and has been absolutely critical to successful implementation.

Our colleagues in Chiang Mai University who are engaged in implementing PBL report similar observations. Since they are at the same institution, they are able to support one another during departmental deliberations and with issues relating to curriculum integration and classroom implementation. Observations of their work style suggest significant changes in the nature of collegial interaction as a positive byproduct of joint implementation.

At this point in time, we have provided formal training to approximately fifty other professors in the use of our model of PBL.

These and other professors who have experience in using PBL can be contacted to answer questions through the PBL discussion group on the Internet. The address for open queries is PBL@ctrvax.vanderbilt.edu. All queries will receive a response.

Institutionalization Stage

This is the stage at which the innovation becomes situated in the organizational routines of the educational institution. Research indicates that institutionalization of educational innovations requires at least three to five years. At this stage, we can observe consistent use of the innovation in the designated curricular domains, formal integration of goals and materials related to the innovation into the preparation curriculum, adjustment in systems of incentives, and adaptation of department policies to reflect the use of the innovation.

Our own experience does not yet qualify us to present a meaningful discussion of the challenges for this stage of the change process with respect to PBL. Bridges' implementation of PBL in the New Pathways to the Principalship program at Stanford begins to approach this stage. However, it still seems premature to provide commentary at this point.

This abbreviated discussion only begins to suggest some of the change issues to consider in the implementation of PBL. The purpose of this chapter is not to engage in an exhaustive review of the change process. Rather it is our intention to foreshadow common implementation issues and highlight practical strategies available to professors. We anticipate that our next book on PBL will focus exclusively on the issues involved in program implementation of problem-based learning.

Closing Thoughts

In reflecting on the content of this book, we are struck by an essential fact that characterizes our experience with problem-based learning. Much of our learning about PBL has resulted from the experience of working with our students. The most salient examples and perspectives on PBL that we provide for readers have been conveyed in the voices of our students.

This, in itself, is testimony to the changed relationship that evolves between the teacher and students in a PBL environment. We draw on the experience and craft knowledge of students as an invaluable resource for mutual learning. We earlier referred to the essays written by our students as part of an "extended conversation" on their learning that unfolds during a course. These data illuminate the students' experience of the learning process and reveal the nature of their metacognitive processing of the content. This feedback is often the basis for new learning on our part as professors that we are then able to share with our students. Consequently, we have drawn extensively on the perspectives of our students throughout the volume.

In practice, we and our colleagues find students' learning in PBL as revealed in their work products to be persuasive data in forming our judgments about the method's efficacy. Both the content and form of students' insights demonstrate the potential power of PBL for achieving important goals in leadership education.

Accordingly, we close the book with reflections on PBL from a student. Jinx Bohstedt is a "weekend" student in Vanderbilt's Ed.D. program in school administration. Her exposure to PBL consisted of a single course, Integrated Inquiry, that had been organized around PBL and that also involved students in PBL development. A staff developer for a school system in Tennessee, she expresses elegantly in her own terms why PBL "works" as a way of learning. This reflection was drawn intact from an integrative essay that she completed at the end of the course.

I have been trying to figure out what makes PBL "work" so well. I know that it works for me because since the class [ended one and a half months ago], I have created two PBL [projects] for summer conferences which I will facilitate. The form and process of PBL seemed to fit with my ideas on teaching. Let's see why.

No matter which way the educational pendulum swings, I have always been a big fan of heterogeneous grouping of students. I think I realized early in my career that some of the students who were not the "A" students offered the deepest insights when solving problems, that the kids who were shy, if offered inviting conditions, would dare nudge the learning of the more assertive and predictable "superior" students. So, for nearly every teaching episode I engaged in, I pondered how to make a single challenging lesson which worked for the variously abled learners, styles of learners and different interests of students. I thought that if I could invent a form [of instruction] that asked for a great span of responses, but maintained the integrity of the concept I wanted them to practice, I might be able to tap into the students' personal styles and interests. [During the course] I used to query [concerning PBL], "How can such a rigid form allow and invite this tremendous creativity?"

Now, I do not think that PBL offers us a "rigid" form; nevertheless it is a form, a protocol which is an organizing device above all. And that is the beauty of it. I believe that it is a resilient form, flexible enough to accommodate different kinds of concepts and different types of learners. Its simple elegance is in providing a universal problem and then offering an invitation to solve it in a personal or specific way. That tension between the universal and the particular is compelling for learners, for it offers a way to connect the unknown to the known self—a powerful teaching and learning strategy.

The invitation to explore various solutions to the problem is inherent in this PBL format; therefore, there is no sense that there is one "right" answer. Nevertheless, one assumes that a high standard will be used to assess [student outcomes]: Were appropriate resources consulted? Did the response have integrity for the problem it solved? Was the communication of the problem's solution clear and persuasive? These attributes and standards are appropriate for learners who bring a wealth of experiences, practiced skills, problem-solving capabilities, and intuition to learning. In no way is PBL patronizing; nor does it play the "guessing game," that is, [I'm the teacher] "I know something you don't know. . . can you figure it out?"

This idea of an organizing form for ALL students' learning within a community of learners seemed central when I taught primary students, and now I see it as compelling for adult learners. The flexibility of the form for divergent responses makes the learner more empowered and the teacher more a facilitator than a "know-all." This serves as a motivating notion for learners to get better and better, and to dig more deeply [into the content].

One last thought on why PBL "works." I have always believed that a large part of teaching is in what happens before and after one works with students. That is, I believe that the selection and preparation of materials before teaching is critical to the success of a lesson. I believe that the assessment of the students' learning experience must be done thoroughly and thoughtfully. PBL essentially carves out the problem, offers numerous resources, and then allows the teacher to step back and out of the way of the subsequent learning. So, in fact, what's different from other forms of teaching or teaching strategies is that the teacher is not central to the moment of contact between student and material, but is central to the learning by preparing rich materials and giving feedback to the individual learner, two realms of the teaching/learning process that we often don't emphasize.

PBL is a powerful and persuasive teaching/learning process. It may help teachers organize concept learning, which is traditionally very elusive. As a process, it certainly manifests the attributes of what makes good teaching: manageable objectives, guiding questions, relevant resources, work with colleagues in a problem-solving atmosphere, a link to the present or known, all of which provide meaning and relevance for the learner, and all of which offer an inherent invitation or challenge to learn. (Jinx Bohstedt, May 1994)

BECAUSE WISDOM CANNOT BE TOLD

A Project for Introducing Problem-Based Learning in Higher Education

Developed by
Edwin M. Bridges • Stanford University
Philip Hallinger • Vanderbilt University and Chiang Mai University

General Instructions

1. Suggested procedures for the session:

    • Read the project description that follows.

    • Discuss the problem in your group, using the roles as described below.

    • Review and discuss the resource materials included with the project in relation to the problem presented in the project.

    • Discuss the guiding questions and complete the product.

    • Present oral reports (described under product specifications).

    • Complete the assessment.

2. One person at your table will serve as the leader of the project; a second will serve as the facilitator; a third will serve as recorder. Determine who will fill these roles as follows:

    Leader, the person with the smallest hand size

    Facilitator, the person with the largest shoe size

    Recorder: the person whose birthday is closest to today (or the person with the second smallest hand size)

Role Definitions

Leader: Primarily responsible for organizing the project in order to accomplish the learning objectives and to complete the product. In the leader role, you:

- Provide initial direction and set the agenda (assign roles, tasks, and time allotments).

- Contribute your own ideas and views about the content of the discussion.

- Do not dominate the meeting; let the facilitator run the meeting.

Facilitator: Acts as the traffic-cop for the group. Keeps group on task and on schedule; helps group to reach consensus (not agreement on what is the best decision but agreement on a decision that everyone can live with). When acting as the facilitator, strive to follow the following guidelines:

- Do not evaluate or contribute ideas to the content of the discussion.

- Contribute your idea only if you signal that you are stepping temporarily out of your role as facilitator.

- Protect individuals and their ideas from personal attack.

- Encourage everyone to participate and do not allow anyone to dominate the discussion.

Recorder: Acts as the group's memory; records major ideas and decisions reached; presents the group's report. When carrying out the role of recorder, please strive to:

- Record the words of the speaker.

- Listen for key words and try to capture basic ideas, the essence of what they say.

- Write down key phrases rather than every word, but don't substitute your ideas for those of the speaker.

- Check periodically to ensure that you are writing what is meant by the speakers.

Problem-Based Learning in Higher Education: A Strategy for Facilitating the Application of Knowledge

"So he had grown rich at last, and thought to transmit to his only son all the cut-and-dried experience which he himself had purchased at the price of his lost illusions; a noble last illusion of age."

This quote vividly highlights the difficulty that people experience in transmitting knowledge to others. In 1940, Charles L. Gragg published an article on management education in which he asserted that "the goal of education is to prepare students for action." The problem of knowledge transfer is particularly acute in the professions where the application of knowledge is paramount (for example, education, law, medicine, administration).

Yet, there has been a growing recognition that professional education has fallen short of the demands of the workplace. Graduates view the content of preparation programs as irrelevant to their work roles. Theory and research appear unrelated to practice. Studies confirm the belief that knowledge and skills gained in professional education often transfer poorly to the workplace. Students often forget much of the material they have learned and/or are unsure how to apply the knowledge they have retained. Moreover, professional education programs have generally ignored the affective domain of education despite its importance in the practice of many professional fields.

The challenge of preparing students for the workplace has taken on increased importance over the past decade as research continues to generate new knowledge at increasing rates. The explosion of knowledge and the use of more efficient information technologies have placed a greater premium on life-long learning as a legitimate goal of professional education. In most professional fields, important curricular domains have changed substantially over the past decade; change in the knowledge base among the professions is likely to accelerate in the future.

Professional preparation programs must increase their capacity to make both current and future knowledge accessible to practitioners. One potential vehicle for closing the gap between our aspirations for student learning and the reality of application is problem-based learning. This approach holds promise for making education more meaningful and for increasing students' ability to access and apply knowledge outside the classroom. In this project, you will have the opportunity to learn about problem-based learning by participating in the process of problem-based learning. It is hoped that you will learn about PBL in a manner that enables you to apply your knowledge to the development of your own educational program.

The Problem

Assume that your educational institution is experiencing a 10 percent cutback in its budget. Further assume that your Dean has conducted a thorough review of each department. Her review reveals that the enrollments in your department show a downward trend over the past four years and that graduates of your program are extremely critical of the quality of their preparation. They maintain that the content lacks any relevance to professional practice and that the instructors rely much too heavily on two methods of instruction: lecture and teacher-led discussion.

The Dean shares her review with your Department Head and asks your department to develop a plan that responds to the declining enrollments and student criticisms. Unless your department comes up with a reasonable plan, it is in danger of suffering a much larger cut than 10 percent and being phased out or merged with another program.

Your Department Head has created three subcommittees to look into problem-centered instructional strategies: case method, case incident technique, and problem-based learning (PBL). You have been assigned to the subcommittee investigating PBL.

The Department Head has charged your subcommittee with reviewing the literature on PBL and preparing a brief report on what you have learned about PBL. You won't have time during this session to draft the report, but you will make a presentation to the other faculty in your department.

Learning Objectives

1. What is PBL and what is the rationale behind its use?

2. How is PBL organized for the classroom and what is the role of students?

3. What is the role of the instructor in PBL?

4. How does PBL operate in a classroom setting?

Guiding Questions

1. What are the major differences between the role of a student in PBL and in the traditional and case methods of instruction?

2. What are the major differences between the role of an instructor in PBL and in the traditional and case methods of instruction?

3. What facets of problem-based learning foster transfer of learning to the workplace?

4. What are some of the advantages and disadvantages of PBL from the teacher's perspective? From the student's perspective?

[Note: The guiding questions are designed to orient you to important knowledge, principles, and issues in the project. It is not intended that you will answer these questions explicitly.]

Product Specifications

1. Prepare an oral report that you will deliver to the rest of your department's instructional staff; this report should indicate:

   a. What you have learned about PBL that is probably of greatest importance to your staff

   b. What the department should do next concerning PBL (for example, drop the idea of using PBL; study the idea in more depth, noting what you want to know more about; use PBL on a limited, trial basis)

   c. Why you are making the recommendation

Each group will have a maximum of fifteen minutes to present its oral report to the other staff in your department. Assume that the people sitting at the table nearest you are the other staff in your department. Be prepared to answer questions of the staff. When one group has completed its presentation and answered questions, the other group should make its presentation.

Resources

For this PBL project, you will have the following resources:

1. Reading materials

   a. Edwin M. Bridges with Philip Hallinger. *Problem-Based Learning for Administrators.* Eugene, Oregon: ERIC Clearinghouse on Educational Management, University of Oregon, 1992. 164 pages. The following sections:

      "PBL: What Is It?" and "PBL: Why Use It?" (pp. 4-13)

      "Introducing Problem-Based Learning to Students" (organization and implementation of PBL) (pp. 19-28)

      "Role of the Instructor in Problem-Based Learning" (pp. 58-64)

      "PBL: What Students Learn" (pp. 65-72, 80-84)

   b. PBL: What the research says about its effectiveness. Albanese, M., and S. Mitchell. "Problem-Based Learning: A Review of the Literature on Its Outcomes and Implementation Issues." *Academic Medicine* 68, 1 (January 1993): pp. 52-81.

   c. C. Gragg. "Because Wisdom Can't Be Told." *Harvard Alumni Bulletin*, October 19, 1940. Reprinted by Harvard Business School, # 451-005.

Although each of you has been provided with all the materials, we encourage you to jigsaw the readings. That is, have each person read one piece or section and then discuss what she or he has read. If more than one person reads the same piece, one person reports and the others offer additional comments if this seems necessary or appropriate. Ordinarily, students read the resource material outside class. Divide up the readings as you see fit given the varying lengths of the selections. If you finish reading your assigned piece, feel free to browse through the book or read one of the other pieces listed above.

2.   Your instructors will be available during the session to answer questions.

3.   As often is the case, one or more group members will have read about the topic or will have had firsthand experience with it. We encourage you to exploit whatever resources exist within your group. [In PBL, students, as well as instructors, serve as resources to the team.]

4.   Videotape: "Can We Make a Better Doctor?" The American public television series NOVA produced this video about the New Pathways Program —a problem-based-learning track—at Harvard University Medical School. This may be viewed by some or all members of the subcommittee as time permits.

Assessment: Talk Back

We need your reactions to this PBL project; these will play an important role in our decisions (that is, modify, leave as is, drop) about this project. Please let us have your candid reactions to what has occurred. We will take them seriously. Please continue your comments on the back of this sheet if necessary.

1. What was the most important thing you learned in today's session?

2. What questions do you have from today's session that remain unanswered?

3. How might this session be changed to make it more useful? (Please be as specific as possible.)

Notes on Project Writing

by Sara Corbett

Go out of your way to avoid vague usage, particularly the passive voice. Consider the following sentence (random example): "This problem was resolved for seven children when a connection was made with an agency that was able to provide replacement glasses." While there is nothing wrong with this statement, it could become more efficient, informative, and engaging through the replacement of vague terms with specifics and the passive voice with the active voice.

As you go through your drafts, try to identify vague words, phrases, and ideas. Pose questions to them. For example: How was the problem resolved? By whom? Who made the connection and how? What is the name of the agency? How was it able to provide replacement glasses? Next step: rewrite your sentence, including as many of the specifics as you can without overloading the sentence or relaying frivolous information. You may break the original sentence into two or even three shorter, clearer ones. "Gloria Diggs, one of the school counselors, contacted the local optometrist who offered fifty new pairs of eyeglasses to the school. Unfortunately, nearly three months passed before the replacement glasses arrived, furthering the academic troubles of the student who couldn't see properly." In the context of the larger problem, this amount of detail is probably not needed for a minor point. However, detail is important. It keeps the reader engaged in your project, so it's one of your best tools for effectively communicating your main ideas.

Characterize when possible. Remember we are looking for a realistic, interesting "story." Your problems, thus, should be peopled by realistic, interesting characters. Consider naming specific characters after endowing them with a bit of personality. This will inspire your reader to "invest" more in the problem. Roger's "Ms. Arthur" is a great example of an engaging character. She's presented through revealing details. She essentially disregards the principal's directive for weekly reports. Not only does she make up a generic schedule for herself, she includes the other counselors in it and takes it upon herself to distribute copies to all the teachers. She later cries, a moment that reminds us these are human issues we are dealing with. All this says quite a bit about who she is, doesn't it? It also validates the principal's hesitancy to deal with her directly throughout the problem.

Give your towns and characters names and personalities. Rather than writing "Some teachers feel this way and others feel another way," consider identifying different factions specifically. Give your situation as much life as possible!

Create a sense of urgency. What's at stake in your problem? What situation or development puts our problem-solver at a point of no return, where the issues absolutely demand to be addressed? For instance, in Bill's problem, the view from friend, coupled with the impending meeting and escalation of complaints from parents and the district office, act as catalysts for change. Given what we're told in the problem, we understand that we must grapple with the issues NOW. Apply this to your PBL project. Have you made clear what's at stake? Are there details, scenarios, external pressures you could add to heighten the PBL participants' adrenaline level?

The problem should be swampy, but your sentences don't need to be. Writing a first and even second draft is all about getting your ideas down and shaping the story. The final revision process involves fine-tuning of not only your ideas, but the language with which you present them as well. Take a hard look at each sentence and then each paragraph. See if you can move or replace words to make your sentences more straightforward. Are you restating a single idea three sentences in a row? Combine, shorten, eliminate where you can. This might buy you space in the places where you need to separate, expand, or elaborate.

Choose lively language. You have countless options when it comes to word choice. Pick the most interesting, most descriptive words (particularly verbs) possible. A good editing exercise is to go through your document and circle every use of the verb "to be." Then go back and replace as many as possible with new words, even if it means rearranging the entire paragraph.

Look again at your introductions. By necessity, they will differ somewhat in basic format from the body of your problem, but the fact that they're summations of a general situation doesn't need to restrict your freedom in word choice. Also consider fiddling with the tense—switch from past to present—and person—from third person to second—just to see if it adds immediacy to your problem.

Organizational Change and Development

Undergraduate - HR 1300

Peabody College • Vanderbilt University • Spring 1995

Instructor:	Dr. Philip Hallinger	Classroom - Payne
Address:	Box 514, Peabody College	Class Sessions:
Telephone:	(615) 343-7092	Office - Payne 205b

Overview

This core course is designed for students who desire preparation for a range of leadership positions in organizations. The primary focus will be on the development of capacities for understanding and bringing about change in organizations. The course will focus on issues of personal, professional, and organizational change.

We will cover a range of topics including change in individuals, change as it concerns work roles in organizations, change as it occurs in the context of small groups, leadership and managerial roles in initiating and implementing change, and the process of change as it unfolds in organizations. The course will afford students the opportunity to: (1) learn new concepts concerning personal, professional, and organizational change; (2) apply learnings in the areas of leadership and small-group processes from prior courses; and (3) develop a more advanced understanding of how that knowledge is applied in practice.

The course will rely largely on problem-based learning as the mode of instruction. This decision is based on the promise afforded by problem-based learning in preparing students for managerial roles. A major goal of the course is for you to learn in ways that increase your ability to understand and apply theoretical and empirical findings concerning change. The general elements of the approach that will be used are as follows.

Principles of Problem-Based Learning

Problem-based learning rests on six principles. These principles and related program features differentiate this approach from other methods of administrative training.

1. Educational objectives and activities should be based on the knowledge and skills needed to address problems encountered in the field, rather than on discrete competencies.

The content of managerial education should deal with major problems that administrators face. For each problem, subject matter and skills that are relevant to dealing with these problems are identified. By using these problems as the focal point for learning, education should become more meaningful and relevant, since the content is potentially useful in solving problems faced by school leaders. Students will be more likely to draw on their training, because the content is stored in memory in relation to the problems for which they are applicable. The ability to retain and transfer knowledge and skills is enhanced by the opportunity for students to apply the training and to receive feedback on their efforts.

2. Teaching should be collaborative.

Instructional resources should include clinicians as well as experts drawn from a variety of disciplines. This increases the ability to simultaneously address knowledge derived from research and theory and knowledge derived from practice.

3. Learning should be largely self-directed by the learner.

Students, not the instructor, should assume major responsibility for guiding and directing their own learning. In the fast-paced world of organizations, administrators seldom have all the necessary resources for solving the problems that arise. The effective leader is able to identify, obtain, and use relevant human and material resources to solve problems.

The instructional staff creates each problem-centered learning module and directs students to *some* of the available resources that may be used in addressing the problem. A block of time is set aside for each module; students then make most of the decisions that arise in relation to dealing with the problem. This includes identification, management, and use of resources. Most decision-making is done in task groups led by the students. Initiative, resourcefulness, and practice in making informed decisions are skills that we hope students will develop through the course.

4. Development experiences should emphasize cooperation and teamwork.

The essence of managerial work is being able to accomplish results through people. This is becoming even more true as schools move increasingly toward site-based management and increase teachers' involvement in decision-making. All modules require students to work in task groups. On some occasions, the group's work will culminate in a group product; on other occasions, participants will draw on the resources of the group to assist in completing individual products.

Leadership of task groups will be rotated among members. It is hoped that each student will have an opportunity to lead a task group for at least a portion of a module. As group leader, the student is responsible for organizing and scheduling its work and for solving problems that arise in relation to group functioning and accomplishment of tasks. Given the scope of work associated with each problem, the group will have to develop a division of labor and rely on its members to fulfill their obligations.

5. Educational experiences should emphasize implementation as well as analysis and reflection.

Traditional case approaches ask participants to describe what they would do if they faced a particular problematic situation. In this course you will be asked to analyze *and* respond to the problematic situation; to the extent possible, you will be asked to execute your plan.

6. Evaluation of students should emphasize diagnostic feedback.

Administrators are often physically isolated from superordinates and peers. This limits the amount of feedback that they typically receive on their performance. Therefore, administrators must develop the capacity to make reasonable self-assessments on-the-job. Traditional university teaching emphasizes summative evaluation (that is, assessment for the purpose of assigning a grade) from one external source —the instructor. Assessment in the course emphasizes diagnostic feedback from multiple sources: peers, the instructor, and, at times, practitioners. Reflective writing exercises will be used to assist students in developing the ability to assess and diagnose their own performance and to set personal learning objectives.

Problem-Based Learning in Practice

These principles and the content of the course will be implemented through a series of PBL *projects*. Each project will typically incorporate the following features:

1. a concrete, specific **problem** that commonly arises in relation to one of the major tasks faced by administrators

2   a set of **guiding questions** to be considered in relation to the problem

3. a set of **reading materials** that shed light on the general task, the specific problem, and the guiding questions

4. a teaching cadre of **professors and clinicians/administrators** who have expertise related to the problem and are willing to act as resources rather than as lecturers

5. **formative evaluation** that provides diagnostic feedback to students

The problems around which the PBL projects are organized represent the content focus for the course. In addition to this content focus, however, there is also an intention to develop managerial skills necessary to function effectively as a school leader. Additional information on the course goals are provided below. (*Note*: specific skill and content objectives will be provided as a part of each learning module.)

Course Goals

1. To expose the student to the important conceptual and practical issues in concerning the change process as experienced by individuals and in organizations;

2. To introduce the student to a perspective on the role of managers that highlights their important leadership tasks, including the centrality of creating conditions that promote

the professional development, personal and organizational effectiveness, and the satisfaction of staff;

3. To equip the student with the specialized knowledge and generic skills (for example, problem-solving, meeting management, memo writing, oral presentation) which are congruent with a leadership perspective on organizational change and development;

4. To give student the opportunity to experience the process of personal change and reflect on the implications for leading change efforts that target other people.

Expectations and Standards

As noted above, this course is designed to assist you in developing a variety of skills, knowledge, and attitudes concerning organizational leadership. The emphasis on group work places greater responsibility on each student to examine his or her performance as a team member. It is my expectation that the course will provide an opportunity for students to assess their strengths and weaknesses as both leaders and followers.

Required Reading

Readings for the course will include:

- E. Bridges and P. Hallinger, *Problem-Based Learning for Administrators*

- Doyle and Straus, *How to Make Meetings Work*

- D. Keirsey, *Please Understand Me*

- a Classpak of readings (available from the instructor)

Students will make their own decisions as to which of the resources they wish to use in completing the learning modules. *Students may wish to draw upon resources other than those provided by the instructor in addressing the learning modules (for example, speak to colleagues, obtain other readings). Students are encouraged to do so.* As a leader your success will depend, in part, on your ability to identify and use resources effectively. Thus, you are free to discuss the case with colleagues outside your task group.

Products

The products for this course vary with each learning module. They will be described in the instructional materials provided by the instructor. Each student will be expected to complete the specified product and a reflective essay for each learning module. Certain modules will also include a knowledge-review exercise.

Grading

The emphasis in this class will be on providing students with ongoing *formative* feedback (that is, diagnosis of strengths and weaknesses) on your performance, rather than on summative feedback (that is, grades). Grades for the course will be determined as a result of three factors: (1) class participation, (2) group work products, and (3) individual work products.

Class Participation: 50%

Class participation will consist of (1) attendance, (2) quality of your group participation, and (3) reflection upon your participation in your group in the form of four *short* (two-page typed, double-spaced) reflective essays.

Individual Work Products: 25%

Some of the class units will have specific activities that will generate an individual product. In other cases, there will be a quiz or test.

Group Work Products: 25%

Each of the units in the course will result in your group generating a group product. These will be graded and you will receive the grade of your group.

The bottom line for the class is that if you don't come to class, you can't participate. If you can't participate, you will have a difficult time excelling in this course. Moreover, since your work and grades will be linked to other members of the groups of which you are a part, sporadic attendance will also adversely affect the grades of other students. Therefore, it is highly recommended that you come to class and participate thoughtfully.

Course Topics and Tentative Class Schedule

Session #1:   *Overview of Course: Personality Type and Leadership*

Session #2:   *Personality Type and Leadership*

Session #3:   *Personality Type and Leadership*

Session #4:   *Because Wisdom Cannot Be Told: Intro to Problem-Based Learning*

Session #5:   *Because Wisdom Cannot Be Told: Intro to Problem-Based Learning*

Session #6:   *Because Wisdom Cannot Be Told: Intro to Problem-Based Learning*

Session #7:   *Because Wisdom Cannot Be Told: Intro to Problem-Based Learning*

Session #8:   *Building Trust in Groups: Roles Exercise*

Session #9:   *Meeting Management and Small Group Processes*

Session #10:   *Meeting Management and Small Group Processes*

Session #11   *Meeting Management and Small Group Processes*

Session #12:   *Meeting Management and Small Group Processes*

Session #13:   *Meeting Management and Small Group Processes*

Session #14:   *Meeting Management and Small Group Processes*

Session #15:   *Personal Processes in Organizational Change*

Session #16:   *Leadership Supporting Change in Individuals and Small Groups*

Session #17:   *Leadership Supporting Change in Individuals and Small Groups*

Session #19:   *Leadership Supporting Change in Individuals and Small Groups*

Session #20:   *Leadership Supporting Change in Individuals and Small Groups*

Session #21:   *Leadership Supporting Change in Individuals and Small Groups*

Session #22:   *Leadership Supporting Change in Individuals and Small Groups*

Session #23:   *Personal Processes in Organizational Change*

Session #24:   *Leading Change in Organizations*

Session #25:   *Leading Change in Organizations*

Session #26:   *Leading Change in Organizations*

Session #27:   *Leading Change in Organizations*

Session #28:   *Leading Change in Organizations*

Session #29:   *Leading Change in Organizations*

Session #30:   *Personal Processes in Organizational Change*

Readings

Personality Type and Leadership

Auerbach, E. (1992, January 6). "Not Your Type, But Right for the Job." *Wall Street Journal.*

Keirsey, D., and Bates, M. (1984). *Please Understand Me.* Del Mar, California: Prometheus Books.

Guild, P. (1987). *Leadership: Examining the Elusive.* Chapter 6, "How Leaders' Minds Work."

Mitroff, I., and Mitroff, D. (1979). "Interpersonal Communication for Knowledge Utilization." *Knowledge Creation, Diffusion, Utilization* 1(2), 203-17.

Problem-Based Learning and Change in Higher Education

Bridges, E., and Hallinger, P. (1992). *Problem-Based Learning for Administrators.* Eugene, Oregon: ERIC Clearinghouse on Educational Management. Selected chapters.

Gragg, C. (1940 , October 19.). "Because Wisdom Cannot Be Told." *Harvard Alumni Bulletin.* Reprinted Harvard Business School, # 451-005.

Hall, G., and Hord, S. (1987). "The Teacher's Point of View: Stages of Concern." *Change in Schools.* New York: SUNY Press.

Meeting Management and Small Group Processes

Author unknown. *Learning to Cooperate: Cooperating to Learn.* Mimeographed.

Author unknown. *Methods of voting*.

Bridges, E. (no date). "Consensus Decision-Making Techniques." Mimeographed.

Cohen, E. (1986). "The Dilemma of Groupwork." In *Designing Groupwork*. New York: Teachers College Press. Pp. 20-33.

Doyle, M., and Straus, D. (1976). *How to Make Meetings Work: The Interaction Method*. New York: Playboy Paperbacks.

Grove, A. (1985). "Meetings." In *High Output Management*. New York: Vintage Books.

Janis, I., and Mann, C. *Groupthink* (selections).

Leithwood, K. (no date). "How Expert School Leaders Solve Swampy Problems in Collaboration with Others." OISE, mimeographed.

Leadership Supporting Change in Individuals and Small Groups

Hersey, P., and Blanchard, K. (1992). *Management of Organizational Behavior*. Fifth Edition. Englewood Cliffs, New Jersey: Prentice Hall. Chapters 8, 10, and 11.

Reimold, C. (1984). *How to Write a Million Dollar Memo*. New York: Dell Publishing. Pp. 1-5, 11-14, 39-45, 90-94.

Sweetnam, S. *The Executive Memo*. Pp. 64-67, 74-82.

Leading Change in Organizations

Crandall, D., Eiseman, J., and Louis, K.S. (1986). "Strategic Planning Issues That Bear on the Success of School Improvement Efforts." *Educational Administration Quarterly* 22 (3), 21-53.

Fullan, M. (1991). *The New Meaning of Educational Change*. New York: Teachers College Press. Chapters 3 (pp. 30-43) and 5 (pp. 65-79).

Hall, G., and Hord, S. (1987). *Change in Schools*. Albany, New York: SUNY Press. Chapters 1 (pp. 23-51), 3 (pp. 52-79), 4 (pp. 80-106).

McLaughlin, M., and Marsh, D. (1978). "Staff Development and School Change." *Teachers College Record*. Pp. 70-94.

Project Planning Form

Project _____

Start: _____   Finish: _____

Purpose:

Problem/Idea/Summary: Goals:

_____   _____

_____   _____

_____   _____

_____   _____

Plan: Main Steps: Time Required: _____

_____

_____

_____

PROJECT RESOURCES
Persons, Contacts, Services: _____

_____

_____

Materials: Readings, Videos, other: _____

_____

_____

Budget: Expenses (if applicable): _____

_____

_____

_____

E

March 25, 1994

To: Students in HRD 1300
From: Dr. Philip Hallinger
Re: Feedback on Your Memos of 3/22/94 Concerning Dorothy
          Wilson

I want to clarify the criteria used to assess your memos concerning *Helen's Awkward Problem*. I will focus here on general issues with respect to the content and form of the memos. Note that the criteria used in my assessments are the same as contained in the *protocols* included in your resource materials.

I have responded separately with respect to your individual memos. My feedback may seem overly *picky* and appear to seek an overly comprehensive approach to the memo. However, I urge you to remember that someone's job is at stake here. Organizations and people tend to take these situations most seriously. Thus, as a supervisor, you must take great care in how you approach them.

Format of Your Memo

A central objective of the assignment was for you to learn how to write a memo that effectively *communicates* your ideas. The product for this project was a memo in which you were expected to communicate with—not simply inform—your supervisor about a difficult problem and how you intend to address it.

Thus, I read your memo first from the perspective of Betsy Graham, keeping in mind whether you fulfilled *her* needs (see Reimhold) with respect to the situation, as opposed to simply informing her as to what happened. I then read your memo from my perspective as your instructor to examine *how* you communicated your ideas.

Point of View

A key element of an effective memo is write it to fulfill the needs of the reader. Some of you simply assumed that by informing Betsy of the problem, you were doing enough. Not!!! The memo is a tool to inform her, get her support in solving the problem in the short- and long-term, demonstrate your competence, and obtain her input as needed. Remember, you are quite new in the organization; *if* it becomes necessary to sanction Dorothy, as a newcomer you will need to have some credibility. After all, this is a problem that others have been content to ignore in the past! As Reimhold notes, you must keep in mind several questions:

- **Who will read the memo?** Your supervisor, Betsy Graham.

- **Why should she?** Because she, presumably, is interested in issues of the Center's productivity and sensitive to problems that could get out of control and reflect on her performance.

- **What problems/needs of hers does it answer?** Potentially, her needs to mentor others (that is, you), to look good to her boss, to avoid problems with other agencies (for example, Dr. Morgan's), to improve productivity.

- **How does it answer a need of hers?** By identifying the problem in a manner that gives her confidence that it will be addressed systematically, within the organization's procedures, with her assistance/support, and leading to an outcome that reduces *other* problems and improves performance of the Center.

Thus, Betsy will read your memo with at least some of the following issues in mind. Did you clearly identify the nature of the problem? Did you document the problem with specific behaviors? Did you address the types of questions that she, as a supervisor, would be concerned with (for example, legal constraints, impact on relations with outside agencies, impact on performance of other workers)? Did you present a clear plan of action with specific steps? Did you recognize and plan for contingencies if your initial plan fails? Was your plan of action consistent with your definition of the problem (many of you recommended actions that were not consistent with your analysis, at least in terms of SLT)? Do you provide a way for Betsy to assist without overburdening her or placing your responsibility on her shoulders?

Also, something that I believe many of you overlooked, the memo is a piece of the *official organizational record* concerning Dorothy's performance. This means it must be written with great care since it could be used as part of a grievance or court proceeding if Dorothy had to be fired or demoted and chose to contest it.

Also, as I suggested earlier, the memo should be used as a means of building support for your course of action with Betsy. Betsy has conflicting issues at work here. She is likely both to want improved performance and to avoid problems. You are new; Dorothy has been around a while. She will definitely do an informal cost-benefit analysis in her head when this problem comes to her desk (that is, in the memo). Is dealing with this problem worth the headaches it could potentially cause for me? For the organization? How much confidence do I have in Helen's ability to deal with this in an effective manner? Thus, your memo also serves to *communicate* a lot of hidden info to Betsy concerning the situation, your role, and hers.

Techniques

1. Did You Frontload Your Ideas?

Important points need to be identified up front, not buried. In this case, the subject title should have specifically indicated the nature of the memo. For example, you might have written: "Re: Action Plan to Improve Performance of Dorothy Wilson." The point is that you want to draw Betsy's attention to the importance and nature of the memo from the outset. Frontloading also involves starting the first paragraph with a clear statement of the problem and your intention.

2. Did You Focus on the Reader?

The memo should be written to "you" as opposed to a third person. This makes it a personal communication rather than an impersonal one, and thereby engages Betsy.

3. Did You Use the Reader's Logic?

Betsy will want to know quickly what the nature of the memo is and the action you have planned. Only then will she be interested in the rationale and history, not the reverse! Otherwise, I can assure you that she will skim to find out the key information (to her) — the action to be taken — because this will shape how she reads the rest of the memo.

4. Did You Make the Memo Readable?

- Did you use short paragraphs?

- Did you use white space to set off the written information?

- Did you use bullets, headers, bold type, underlining, and other stylistic tools to highlight and organize your ideas?

5. Did You Use Clear, Nontechnical Language?

Don't assume that your supervisor knows anything about situational leadership. Your task was to communicate how you saw the problem and what you proposed to do. Clear language with an absence of jargon is the appropriate way to do this. Note that nothing in your instructions for the assignment directed you to use the jargon of SLT *in the memo*. In fact, that was why I asked you to indicate the thinking behind your memo in terms of SLT in a separate attachment written to me.

These techniques should have helped you attain your goal of communicating effectively with Betsy, your supervisor. Of course, in addition to the format of your memo, I was also concerned with its content.

Content of the Memo

The content of your memo should have included:

1. a *definition of the problem* and its ramifications on the Center

2. an *analysis of Dorothy's readiness level* and the group's in terms of specifics, but without the jargon of SLT

3. the *leadership style* you plan to use with her in terms of concrete steps and actions, but again without the jargon of SLT

4. *what you want from Betsy* and the plan for future communication on this subject

Nature of the Analysis

As I noted in class, Dorothy's readiness level is R1. She is in a regressive cycle, and has been for some time. This has been reinforced by the inappropriate use of an S4 leadership style by Lila, her former supervisor. Given this analysis, which is supported by a number of specific facts, an S1 leadership style is appropriate with Dorothy.

Three constraints shape your attempts to address the problem. First, legally, it is likely that you will need to document Dorothy's performance over a period of at least six months. This will vary according to organizational policies and norms, which of course you have researched prior to writing the memo. Also, it is likely that you will not have the authority to fire Dorothy yourself, should that become necessary. Instead, you will need Betsy's support, something that you need to begin to develop now.

Second, because Dorothy's pattern of behavior is longstanding, any improvement plan will need to be comprehensive, coordinated, and persistent. Again, you will need support from above and you will need to work closely with Dorothy over a period of time.

Third, you will need to address Dorothy's coworkers inside and outside the agency. Despite their displeasure with Dorothy, her colleagues have adapted to her behavior. Changing Dorothy's behavior will involve changing *their* patterns of responding to her.

These constraints suggest several responses. First, you will need to sit down with Dorothy, setting clear goals with respect to her tasks and spelling out your expectations for how tasks are to be accomplished (that is, standards for performance). Then you will need to outline a system for monitoring her performance on a regular basis. While this would not be pleasant and Dorothy can be expected to balk, it is necessary in light of her performance. Two-way communication would be kept to a minimum until you begin to see some improvement in performance.

Simultaneously, you need to inform Betsy of your plan. You need to clarify the conditions under which Dorothy's employment can be terminated under the municipality's regulations. Then you must make sure that the steps you take will meet those conditions, if Dorothy's performance does not improve. This will also involve developing support from other actors, in this case, Betsy and perhaps Dr. Morgan.

The group appears to be functioning at an R2 level. While they are responsive, they are lacking some of the group resources needed to solve their problems, specifically with Dorothy. An S2 leadership style appears appropriate at this time in order to help them break the habit of covering for Dorothy and in supporting new norms within the Center. It would also be possible to use an S3 style if you made certain assumptions about their readiness.

See the attached sample memo that I wrote. This illustrates some of the ideas suggested above.

Grading

The grading for this project has three components, each of which will be factored into your semester grade. First, I graded you on the *format* of your memo. This included the stylistic techniques designed to make your memo readable. Format issues also included the degree to which you incorporated a *reader-centered approach*. Was your memo written to inform or communicate?

Second, I graded your project on the *content* of the memo. This assessment examined the extent and manner in which you defined the problem and developed an action plan that was concrete, specific, and reasonable in light of the facts in the case scenario. As suggested earlier, I was interested in a variety of issues concerned with Helen, her relationship to Dorothy, the group, and Betsy. I expected some form of contingency plan, and that your analysis/recommendations would accurately reflect SLT concepts.

Finally, I gave you a third grade that reflected other dimensions of the project. These included your first-draft memo (Did you do one?), the attached assessment of actors in terms of SLT, the integrative essay, your role in the group, and the minicases.

Bibliography

Many of the items in this bibliography are indexed in ERIC's monthly catalog *Resources in Education (RIE)*. Reports in *RIE* are indicated by an "ED" number. Journal articles, indexed in ERIC's companion catalog, *Current Index to Journals in Education,* are indicated by an "EJ" number.

Most items with an ED number are available from ERIC Document Reproduction Service (EDRS), 7420 Fullerton Rd., Suite 110, Springfield, VA 22153-2852.

To order from EDRS, specify the ED number, type of reproduction desired—microfiche (MF) or paper copy (PC), and number of copies. Add postage to the cost of all orders and include check or money order payable to EDRS. For credit card orders, call 1-800-443-3742.

Albanese, M., and S. Mitchell. "Problem-Based Learning: A Review of Literature on Its Outcomes and Implementation Issues." *Academic Medicine* 68, 1 (January 1993): 52-81. EJ 457 739.

Barrows, H. "A Taxonomy of Problem-Based Learning Methods." *Medical Education* 20 (1986): 481-86.

_____. *How to Design a Problem-Based Curriculum for the Preclinical Years.* New York: Springer Publishing Company, 1985.

Barrows, H., and R. Tamblyn. *Problem-Based Learning: An Approach to Medical Education.* New York: Springer Publishing Company, 1980.

Beaty, J. Personal communication, November 7, 1987.

Berman, P., and M. McLaughlin. "Implementation of Educational Innovations." *Educational Forum* 40 (1978): 347-70.

Borg, W., and M. Gall. "Educational Research and Development." In *Educational Research: An Introduction.* Fifth Edition. White Plains, New York: Longman, 1989.

Boud, D., and G. Feletti, *The Challenge of Problem-Based Learning.* New York: St. Martin's Press, 1991.

Bransford, J.; J. Franks; N. Vye; and R. Sherwood. "New Approaches to Instruction: Because Wisdom Can't Be Told." In *Similarities and Analogical Reasoning,* edited by S. Vosniadou and A. Ortony. 470-97. New York: Cambridge University Press, 1989.

Bridges, E. "The Nature of Leadership." In *Educational Administration: The Developing Decades,* edited by L. Cunningham, W. Hack, and R. Nystrand. 202-30. Berkeley, California: McCutchan, 1977.

_____. "Research on the School Administrator: State of the Art, 1967-1980." *Educational Administration Quarterly* 18, 3 (Summer 1982): 12-33. EJ 268 213.

_____. *Time Management: The Work of the Principal.* PBL Project. Instructor's Edition. Eugene, Oregon: ERIC Clearinghouse on Education Management, University of Oregon, 1994. 112 pages.

Bridges, E., and P. Hallinger. "Problem-Based Learning in Medical and Managerial Education." In *Cognitive Perspectives on Educational Leadership,* edited by P. Hallinger, K. Leithwood, and J. Murphy. 253-67. New York: Teachers College Press, 1992.

Bridges, E. M., with P. Hallinger. *Problem-Based Learning for Administrators.* Eugene, Oregon: ERIC Clearinghouse on Education Management, University of Oregon, 1992. 164 pages.

Chenoweth, T., and R. Everhart. "Preparing Leaders to Understand and Facilitate Change: A Problem-Based Learning Approach." *Journal of School Leadership* 4, 4 (1994): 414-31.

Covey, S. *The Seven Habits of Highly Effective People.* New York: Simon and Schuster, 1989.

Cooper, B., and W. Boyd. "The Evolution of Training for School Administrators." In *Approaches to Administrative Training in Education,* edited by J. Murphy and P. Hallinger. 3-27. Albany: State University of New York Press, 1987.

Crowson, R., and B. McPherson. "The Legacy of the Theory Movement: Learning from the New Tradition." In *Approaches to Administrative*

Training in Education, edited by J. Murphy and P. Hallinger. 45-66. Albany: State University of New York Press, 1987.

Doyle, M., and D. Straus. *How to Make Meetings Work.* New York: Jove Books, The Berkeley Publishing Group, 1982 .

Eckholm, M. "Evaluating the Impact of Comprehensive School Leadership Education in Sweden." *Education and Urban Society* 24, 3 (May 1992): 365-85.

Engel, C. "Not Just a Method, but a Way of Learning." In *The Challenge of Problem-Based Learning,* edited by D. Boud and G. Feletti. 23-33. New York: St. Martin's Press, 1991.

Fullan, M. *The New Meaning of Educational Change.* New York: Teachers College Press, 1991.

Fullan, M., and A. Pomfret. "Research on Curriculum and Instruction Implementation." *Review of Educational Research,* 47 (1977): 335-97.

Griffiths, D.; R. Stout; and P. Forsyth. *Leaders for Tomorrow's Schools.* Berkeley, California: McCutchan Publishing Co., 1988.

Habschmidt, B. "Something Old, Something New and the Principal's Blues." Unpublished doctoral dissertation. Nashville, Tennessee: Vanderbilt University, 1990.

Hall, G., and S. Hord. *Change in Schools.* Albany, New York: SUNY Press, 1987.

Hall, M. "Constructivist Educational Theory in Practice: An Analysis of Problem-Based Learning in the Classroom." Unpublished paper. Nashville, Tennessee: Peabody College, 1994.

Hallinger, P. "School Leadership Development: Evaluating a Decade of Reform." *Education and Urban Society* 24, 3 (May 1992): 300-16.

Hallinger, P., and L. Anast. "The Indiana Principals' Leadership Academy: School Reform for Principals." *Education and Urban Society* 24, 3 (May 1992): 410-30. EJ 445 358.

Hallinger, P., and R. Greenblatt. "Principals' Pursuit of Professional Growth: The Influence of Beliefs, Experiences and District Context." *Journal of Staff Development* 10, 4 (Fall 1990): 68-74. EJ 414 185.

Hallinger, P., and B. Habschmidt. *Leadership and School Culture.* PBL Project. Instructor's Edition. Eugene, Oregon: ERIC Clearinghouse on Education Management, University of Oregon, 1994. 160 pages.

Hallinger, P., and J. Murphy. "Developing Leaders for Tomorrow's Schools." *Phi Delta Kappan* 72, 7 (March 1991): 514-20. EJ 422 811.

Jennings, J. "Closing the Achievement Gap." Unpublished doctoral dissertation. Nashville, Tennessee: Vanderbilt University, 1992. ED 356 865.

Joyce, B., and B. Showers. *Power in Staff Development Through Research in Training*. Alexandria, Virginia: Association for Supervision and Curriculum Development, 1983. 50 pages. ED 240 667.

Keirsey, D., and M. Bates. *Please Understand Me*. Del Mar, California: Prometheus Nemesis, 1984.

Margetson, D. "Why Is Problem-Based Learning a Challenge?" In *The Challenge of Problem-Based Learning*, edited by D. Boud and G. Feletti. 42-50. New York: St. Martin's Press, 1991.

Marsh, D. "School Principals as Instructional Leaders: The Impact of the California School Leadership Academy." *Education and Urban Society* 24 (May 1992): 386-410.

McLaughlin, M., and D. Marsh. "Staff Development and School Change." *Teachers College Record* 80, 1 (1978): 69-94.

Munter, M. *Guide to Managerial Communication*. Third edition. Englewood Cliffs, New Jersey: Prentice Hall, 1992.

Murphy, J. *The Landscape of Leadership Development*. Newbury Park, California: Corwin Press, 1993.

Murphy, J., and P. Hallinger. "New Directions in the Professional Development of School Administrators: A Synthesis and Suggestions for Improvement." In *Approaches to Administrative Training in Education*, edited by J. Murphy and P. Hallinger. 245-82. Albany: State University of New York Press, 1987.

Neame, R. "Problem-Based Medical Education: The Newcastle Approach." In *New Directions for Medical Education: Problem-Based Learning and Community Oriented Medical Education.*, edited by H. Schmidt, M. Lipkin, M. de Vries, and J. Greep. 112-47. New York: Springer Verlag, 1989.

Nova. *Can We Make a Better Doctor?* Washington, D. C.: Public Broadcasting System, n.d.

Painvin, C.; V.R. Neufeld; G.R. Norman; and others. "The Triple Jump Exercise—A Structured Measure of Problem-Solving and Self-Directed Learning." In *Proceedings of the 18th Conference of Research in Medical Education*. Washington, D. C., 1979.

Parks, D. "Issues in Curriculum and Instruction in Preparation Programs for Educational Leaders." *Connections!* 2, 2 (1994): 4-5, 11.

Pigors, P. *The Pigors Incident Process of Case Study.* New Jersey: Educational Technology Publications, 1980.

Swanson, D.; S. Case; and C. van der Vleuten. In *The Challenge of Problem-Based Learning,* edited by D. Boud and G. Feletti. New York: St. Martin's Press, 1991.

Sweetnam, S. *The Executive Memo.* New York: Wiley, 1986.

Walton, H., and M. Matthews. "Essentials of Problem-Based Learning." *Medical Education* 23 (1989): 542-58.

Waterman, R.; P. Akmajian; and S. Kearny. *Community-Oriented Problem-Based Learning at the University of New Mexico.* Albuquerque, New Mexico: University of New Mexico School of Medicine, 1991.

Whitehead, A. *The Aims of Education and Other Essays.* New York: The Macmillan Company, 1929.

Wildman, L. "Where Will LEAD Lead?" *Educational Policy* 3, 3 (1989): 275-87.

Wilkerson, L., and E. Hundert. "Becoming a Problem-Based Tutor: Increasing Self-Awareness Through Faculty Development." In *The Challenge of Problem-Based Learning,* edited by D. Boud and G. Feletti. 159-72. New York: St. Martin's Press, 1991.

Wimpelberg, R. "The Inservice Development of Principals: A New Movement, Its Characteristics, and Future." In *Advances in Educational Administration,* Vol. 1, edited by P. Thurston and L. Lotto. Greenwich, Connecticut: JAI Press, 1990.

Additional Resources on Problem-Based Learning

A criticism leveled at principal preparation programs is that they fail to give students sufficient practical experience in wrestling with problems they are likely to face once they become school administrators. An innovative instructional strategy called *problem-based learning* (PBL) has caught the attention of those who want to address this shortcoming. The ERIC Clearinghouse on Educational Management has published a variety of resources to help professors make fullest use of this instructional technique.

Problem-Based Learning for Administrators

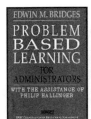

by Edwin M. Bridges with the assistance of Philip Hallinger
1992 • ISBN: 0-86552-117-4
xii + 164 pages • perfect (sew/wrap) bind • $10.95
Professor Bridges spent five years developing, field testing, and refining PBL for use in educational management classes, and this book is the record of what he has learned. Using student essays, detailed descriptions of actual projects, data from PBL in the medical field, and his own observations, Bridges illustrates how PBL teaches leadership, management, and communication skills to administrative students.

PBL Projects: A New Curriculum for Administrator Training

In a PBL environment, instructors present students with problematic situations called *projects*. A project is the basic unit of instruction in a PBL curriculum. Although the problems are simulated, students experience them as real. Working together in small teams, students assume responsibility for responding to the problems they are presented with. Instead of functioning as dispensers of knowledge, PBL instructors serve as observers and advisors.

Time Management: Work of the Principal
by Edwin M. Bridges
1994 • ISBN: 0-86552-122-0 (Instructor Edition)
Text, 57 pages; reading materials, 106 pages
Instructor Edition: $15.00, Student Edition: $14.00
Students participate in a simulation involving a range of activities and problems—handling correspondence, dealing with interruptions, conducting a classroom observation, holding an unscheduled meeting with a hostile parent, and making an oral presentation to a group of concerned parents.

194

Write Right!
by Edwin M. Bridges
1994 • ISBN: 0-86552-125-5 (Instructor Edition)
Text, 19 pages; reading materials, 34 pages
Instructor Edition: $6.00, Student Edition: $5.50
   Since writing is a central communication tool used by principals, principals-in-training must hone their writing skills. This project focuses on organizing, preparing, and editing written communication; it gives special attention to memos, the principal's most frequently used form of written communication.

Leadership and School Culture
by Philip Hallinger and
Barbara L. Habschmidt
1994 • ISBN: 0-86552-123-9 (Instructor Edition)
Text, 21 pages; reading materials, 155 pages
Instructor Edition: $15.50, Student Edition: $14.50
In this project, students face the challenges inherent in a changing school context. It is intended to help principals-in-training gain additional insight into how people respond to change and to learn more about the leader's role in supporting, stimulating, and guiding change within the school environment. Specifically, students are faced with the problem of a veteran school faculty facing multiple changes in their work context over which they feel little control.

Instructor and Student Editions

The authors have created two versions of each project—a student edition and an instructor edition. The instructor edition includes an extra section called a *Teaching Note*, which offers an overview of the project, suggests possible ways of setting the stage for the project, informs instructors of issues that may surface during the course of the project, and recommends topics that instructors may wish to address when offering feedback to students.

For instructors' convenience, project authors have compiled a range of required and optional reading materials for students to review and digest prior to the start of each project simulation. Appearing at the back of each project, these appended materials give students a background of pertinent information to draw from when confronting issues integral to the projects. Fees paid to the copyright holders for reproduction of these materials are included in the price of each project.